THE BUSINESS OF PERSONAL TRAINING

THE BUSINESS OF PERSONAL TRAINING

Essential Guide for the Successful Personal Trainer

ANDREA OH

PHOENIX
Interactive Consulting
Chicago, IL MMXIII

Copyright © 2013 by Andrea Oh. All rights reserved.

Cover Design: M. Masters
Editor: B. Cunningham

Published by: PHOENIX Interactive Consulting, LLC.
 (www.phoenix-interact.com)

All rights reserved. No part of this publication may be reproduced, distributed, or transmitted in any form or by any means, including photocopying, recording, or other electronic or mechanical methods, without the prior written permission of the publisher, except in the case of brief quotations embodied in critical reviews and certain other noncommercial uses permitted by copyright law.

Printed in the United States of America

ISBN 978-1490589626

DEDICATION

To my mother (a woman of undeniable strength and faith) and Bill (for taking a risk on the dark horse).

TABLE OF CONTENTS

List of Tables — i
List of Figures — iii
Foreword — v
Preface — ix
Introduction — xiii

Part One: The Personal Training Opportunity — 1
Chapter 1: Ready. Aim. Fire! — 5
Chapter 2: Getting to Know the Personal Training Industry — 9
Chapter 3: What is Personal Training? — 21
Chapter 4: Reasons Why People Hire Personal Trainers — 27
Chapter 5: 7 Habits of Highly Effective Personal Trainers — 35
Chapter 6: Health Care Reform and the Fitness Industry — 41
Chapter 7: Personal Trainer = Fitness Entrepreneur — 47

Part Two: Building Your Personal Training Business — 53
Chapter 8: Planning for Success — 57
Chapter 9: Getting Certified — 65
Chapter 10: Building Experience — 81
Chapter 11: Creating Your Personal Brand — 89
Chapter 12: Building Your Business — 95
Chapter 13: Marketing Your Brand — 101
Chapter 14: Learning How to Sell — 115
Chapter 15: Protecting Your Business — 125
Chapter 16: Open for Business - The First 90 Days — 137
Chapter 17: Growing Your Business - Specialization — 147
Chapter 18: Growing Your Business - Products and Services — 151
Chapter 19: Final Thoughts — 155

Testimonials — 159

LIST OF TABLES

Table 2-1:	Evolution of Modern Fitness (as portrayed by the media)	15
Table 9-1:	ACTION Personal Trainer Certification	68
Table 9-2:	American College of Sports Medicine (ACSM)	69
Table 9-3:	American Council on Exercise (ACE)	70
Table 9-4:	Canadian Fitness Professionals (CanFitPro)	71
Table 9-5:	International Fitness Professional Association (IFPA)	72
Table 9-6:	International Sports Sciences Association (ISSA)	73
Table 9-7:	National Academy of Sports Medicine (NASM)	74
Table 9-8:	National Council on Strength and Fitness (NCSF)	75
Table 9-9:	National Exercise and Sports Trainers Association (NESTA)	76
Table 9-10:	National Federation of Personal Trainers (NFPT)	77
Table 9-11:	National Personal Training Institute	78
Table 9-12:	National Strength and Conditioning Association (NSCA)	79
Table 16-1:	New Personal Training Business Checklist	145

LIST OF FIGURES

Figure 13-1:	Personalized Business Card	107
Figure 13-2:	Pricing Sheet	108
Figure 13-3:	Client Testimonials	109
Figure 13-4:	Newsletter (Printed or Electronic)	110
Figure 13-5:	Workout/Program Books	111
Figure 13-6:	Business Website	112
Figure 13-7:	Business Social Media	113
Figure 15-1:	Trainer-Client Agreement	131
Figure 15-2:	Waiver of Liability	132
Figure 15-3:	Health Screening Questionnaire	133
Figure 15-4:	Physician Referral Form	134
Figure 15-5:	Letter of Consent for Minors	135

FOREWORD

I had just completed my second book, co-authoring with Brian Tracy, called "Against the Grain: How to Achieve Positive Results in a Down Economy", when Andrea asked If I would write the forward for her book, "The Business of Personal Training".

After my first reaction, being "WOW! I'd be honored.", my mind then began racing through all of the accomplishments I'd witnessed Andrea achieve in the short year we had been working together.

To start, let me lay some groundwork. My company, Today's Growth Consultant, partners with experts, executives, professional athletes, and industry thought leaders on large "authority" websites. We co-own 200+ websites that are viewed over 100,000,000 times each year. Each of our sites is authored by true authority figures in each industry. Andrea authors our fitness authority site, www.todaysfitnesstrainer.com. Here's how this particular site became a reality.

I took a call, just over a year ago, from one of our website investment partners, Bill Cunningham. This is my recollection of this short call.

Bill Cunningham: "Ken. Bill here."

Ken Courtright:		"Hey Bill, how's it going?"
Bill Cunningham:		"Great! Do I remember correctly that you were on the hunt for an authority figure in the area of fitness?"
Ken Courtright:		"Yes. Next to "food" and "insurance", "fitness" is the third hottest industry world-wide."
Bill Cunningham:		"Well ... you can cross off that category and close down that industry. I found her! She's incredible! She's a trainer, a former professional athlete, a writer, a business owner, and a visionary. Her name is Andrea Oh. Just wait until you meet her!"

After five minutes of Bill going on and on, as to how great of a fitness expert Andrea was, I was hooked. Later that day I spent time getting to know Andrea Oh. Like the part in the Jerry McGuire movie, "You had me at 'Hello',", I was completely reeled in within minutes. Andrea's wisdom is extraordinary and her energy is contagious. More importantly, her life's experiences are invaluable to any personal trainer or fitness professional.

In my first book, "Online Income: Navigating the Internet Minefield", I explain that the safest way to walk through a minefield is by following the footprints of others. If you don't see blood, keep going. I could tell within minutes of speaking with Andrea that she possessed experience in battle and had left footprints behind when it came to the world of fitness. By the end of our call, instead of Andrea selling us on why she should be chosen as the writer for what would someday be a very famous fitness site, I felt myself selling Andrea on why she should take a chance on us providing her the platform to help the world understand the value and reach of the fitness industry. Most importantly, I wanted her to realize the impact personal trainers can play in a person's life.

After reading "The Business of Personal Training", I was again reminded of the depth of Andrea's knowledge on the topic. In over twenty years, our company has consulted just over three thousand companies on how to better grow their business. While reading Andrea's manuscript, I found myself earmarking pages to make sure we were counseling businesses on certain growth tips and potential pitfalls Andrea covers in this book.

Andrea takes a new personal trainer on a journey that is priceless. Starting with logical reasoning behind why someone should and should not consider personal training as a career, Andrea provides the literal footprints to becoming a "successful" personal trainer. The theme throughout the book is one of "success". I could literally feel Andrea writing parts of the book knowing these were common areas that new fitness trainers often struggled through.

Andrea goes out of her way to share her life's journey to becoming a successful trainer by providing over two dozen printable aids to make sure a new trainer has all the tools available to be successful. The book includes templates for sales aids, marketing materials and even insurance forms and documents that can literally make or break a fitness trainer's career (if not used properly).

After perfectly covering the importance of a concise business plan, Andrea explains the importance of a good marketing plan, brand message, and website. If that wasn't enough, Andrea provides samples anyone can use as starter templates to guarantee a professional "first impression".

Andrea is an incredible individual that follows the principle:
"A key to success is to continually take your eyes off yourself and keep them on others."

I'm very proud to be in business with Andrea Oh.

Ken Courtright
Founder, Today's Growth Consultant (www.todaysgrowthconsultant.com)
Author, Online Income: Navigating the Internet Minefield

PREFACE

Over the past two decades I've had the pleasure of seeing many sides of the fitness industry. With a passion for competitive sports and physical activity I eagerly pursued a path in school as an exercise physiologist and biomechanist. In other words, I wanted to be a bonafide "fitness nerd". Being the rebel of the family, it wasn't a surprise I chose a path that didn't meet the expectations of my parents (i.e. doctor, accountant, or lawyer). Instead, I pursued a career that added a professional credibility to my love of fitness and exercise.

The first five years in the business were far from "smooth sailing". To be honest, they were tough! Just like the majority of fitness professionals new to the market, I had high hopes and aspirations of greatness. With a positive attitude and lofty goals, I took on a wide variety of jobs to make ends meet (i.e. athletic trainer, group fitness instructor, and personal trainer).

Although I loved the challenge of the job, and made amazing connections with my personal training colleagues and clients, working for someone else would never lead me to accomplishing the goals I wanted to achieve in the industry. I wanted to change the industry and find a way to make fitness more widely accepted.

I could have been content helping my clients make lasting change in their lives but I knew I was meant for bigger things. I knew I wanted to be an innovator and change the industry ... to find ways to make the fitness experience better for people of all ages and abilities.

I also realized that working hard at something doesn't necessarily guarantee positive results. I found myself putting a lot of time and effort into my work and not getting positive results because I was focusing on the wrong things. I was going down the same path most fitness professionals follow, making mistakes that hold them back from true business success. For me, it became very clear that I had to think "outside the box" and make a bold move.

Leaving the fitness club environment, and the industry, for five years was the best thing that I could have done to grow and evolve as a business professional. Although my "day job" wasn't in fitness, I stayed connected to it through volunteer projects and my relationships with peers in the industry. My experiences in a corporate environment gave me new perspectives on health, wellness, and (most importantly) business.

When the time was right I made my way back to fitness, on a mission to establish myself on the "other side" of the industry. Rather than helping one person at a time on the workout floor I wanted to find ways to help hundreds (or thousands) of people be successful in their own mission to help others through fitness. It was scary ... but a challenge worth pursuing.

The next ten years were filled with incredible highs and defeating lows and, in the end, were the greatest years of my learning and growth (as a person and an entrepreneur). I was blessed with the opportunity to apply my knowledge of business strategy, sales process, marketing and promotional initiatives to my own business and other projects. I had the luxury of applying my knowledge and seeing the results, good or bad, each and every day.

Through this process, my biggest regret was not seeking out the help of others in the industry or the people that I trusted to keep my on the right track. I was far too proud and determined to do it on my own. It wasn't until many years later that I humbly admitted this mistake.

Just like many other entrepreneurs, I found myself in situations where I had fallen hard off the horse, looked up at the horse in anger and defiance, wanted badly to just give up and walk away, and then realized the right thing to do was to get back up, dust myself off, and try again.

Although I didn't have the luxury of a true business support system, I managed to survive the tough years and build great companies and strong relationships in business along the way. For this I am truly grateful!

The negative experiences I've endured, and what I learned from each and every one of them, are the reasons why I decided to produce this book. I didn't want others, passionate about pursing a career in fitness, to go through the same obstacles and challenges I did. The fitness industry needs great people who are armed and ready to tackle an overwhelming task ... to get all people healthy and living high quality lives.

With this book, my goal is to help entrepreneurial personal trainers become successful in their business ... the first time out. The industry, as it stands today, doesn't provide personal trainers with the tools to establish a long-lasting business. Personal trainers are on their own if they make the decision to leave their job with a fitness club or private studio and work for themselves.

Today, I can honestly say I am a person who isn't afraid of admitting my mistakes. I guess that's why I was completely at ease writing a book that highlights my epic failures and the learnings that I gained from working through each one. As a business strategist and marketing specialist, I have taken my knowledge and experience and helped numerous fitness companies and organizations improve their business to meet the demands of a fast growing industry.

Regardless of whether you are brand new to the business or have been running your own studio for many years, I believe the information in these pages will provide great value for the reader who is serious about their personal training business.

> I want you to avoid the costly mistakes I (and countless others) have made in the past.
>
> I want you to have the knowledge and experience of someone who has successfully built businesses in the fitness industry from the ground up and helped others thrive.
>
> I want you to take full advantage of the amazing business opportunities available to you through fitness.
>
> I want you to maintain your passion and excitement for helping others improve their lives through physical activity and exercise.
>
> I want you to become an inspiring success story as your own personal training business becomes a reality.

Andrea Oh
Founder, Today's Fitness Trainer (www.todaysfitnesstrainer.com)
Author, The Business of Personal Training: Essential Guide for the Successful Personal Trainer

INTRODUCTION

In 2010, a shift occurred in the fitness industry that couldn't be denied. Several factors brought fitness, wellness and health to the forefront of global awareness (i.e. shocking obesity statistics from the Centers for Disease Control and Prevention and the World Health Organization, television shows like "The Biggest Loser" and "Extreme Weight Loss", and Michelle Obama's "Let's Move" campaign, to name a few). An industry that started out in the 1970s, as a labor of love and a "hobby" for people who enjoyed the fitness experience, was quickly growing up as other industries were starting to take notice.

With the most recent recession (from December 2007 to June 2009), a time where there was a general slowdown in economic activity and higher unemployment rates, the fitness industry was not affected like other industries. In fact, according to the Bureau of Labor 2010-2011 Occupational Outlook Handbook the fitness industry will experience at least a 20 percent growth by 2018.

These events were the "wake up call" that inspired the development of the fitness authority website, www.TodaysFitnessTrainer.com. This authority website was a collaborative effort between Today's Growth Consultant, Bill Cunningham, and myself that, to date, has far exceeded our expectations since its official launch in 2011.

As the Editor-In-Chief of the website, my original goal was to develop a website that would accommodate the needs of fitness professionals looking to advance their careers in fitness. With my background as a group fitness instructor, personal trainer, fitness education developer, and business and marketing strategist, this website would serve as a platform to share useful information in an effort to help fitness instructors and personal trainers improve their own businesses.

Today, it has evolved to a fitness authority website with two audiences:
1. The fitness professional looking to advance their business
2. The non-fitness professional looking for information about fitness in general.

I struggled with this transition for quite some time but then realized that many fitness professionals, like myself, got their start in the industry because of their fitness experiences as a member of a fitness club, a person recovering from an injury, or an athlete wanting to improve their overall performance. I wanted to provide a medium that guided a person along a path from fitness "newbie" to super star personal trainer. I wanted to help people realize the amazing opportunity the fitness industry had to offer anyone wanting to take the "bull by the horns".

This book came about as a result of comments by readers and industry professionals who were looking for the information they read on the site compiled into a single book (a book that outlined the most important information a personal trainer should know when building a successful personal training business). The book was written to help the person thinking about getting into the business in addition to the established personal trainer who was looking to grow and improve their current business.

The original content from www.TodaysFitnessTrainer.com was rewritten, with additional content, to provide readers with the information they were looking for in an easy-to-follow and understandable way.

Our goal with this book (and others currently in development) is to take the best of what www.TodaysFitnessTrainer.com has to share and give people the tools they need to be their own personal trainer success story.

For new personal training articles and information pertaining to the fitness industry, market trends, sales and marketing strategies, visit www.TodaysFitnessTrainer.com. You can subscribe and receive the newest articles in your email Inbox each week. Also, visit our Facebook page at www.facebook.com/TodaysFitnessTrainer for updates on all new content, fitness tips and information that just might surprise you!

THE BUSINESS OF PERSONAL TRAINING

You miss 100 percent of the shots you never take.

~ Wayne Gretzky

PART ONE:
THE PERSONAL TRAINING OPPORTUNITY

Recent studies suggest the average person can expect to change their career three to seven times in their lifetime. This is due to the instability of the job market and the increasing number of people looking for more control and autonomy in the workplace. If you are one of these people, looking for something better, more fulfilling and profitable for yourself (or your family), you may want to consider personal training as your next career!

In fact, you wouldn't be the only one thinking about it. Personal training is a career in high demand because of the demand for preventive health professionals and because of its unique qualities. Personal training is:

- Dedicated to helping people get healthier, be more active and live a better quality of life.
- Part of an industry that will grow by 20% by 2018.
- Motivating, energetic, creative and fun.
- A career that anyone over the age of 18 years can do (with the right education and training).

Why People Change Careers

As adults, the time we dedicate to our career makes up the majority of our time, second to the hours we need for rest, recovery and sleep. Many of us enter into the workforce out of high school, college or

university with little experience and limited choices. Only a few of us get our "dream" job the first time out. We all look for a career that:
- We are passionate about and that we enjoy.
- Involves close, caring relationships with others.
- Provides an opportunity to create something of meaning and value.

We also look for an opportunity that can provide us with an environment where we:
- Feel respected and appreciated.
- Can be successful in our job.
- Have a clear career path and future with the company.
- Have control over our destiny (with hard work and dedication).

If a person's current job situation doesn't fulfill these requirements, the likelihood that they will leave their current place of employment to find something new is high.

Why Personal Training?
A better quality of life is important for all people, young or old, big or small, male or female. We all desire it but the challenge comes from the lack of motivation needed to take the action necessary to be healthier and more fit. According to the Bureau of Labor 2010-2011 Occupational Outlook Handbook the fitness industry will experience at least a 20 percent growth by 2018. It's easy to see why this may be the case when the industry, as a whole, is focused on motivating people to get healthier and more active. The fitness industry is notorious for making money being the "masters of motivation".

A career as a certified personal trainer has become increasingly popular as new fitness clubs and specialty studios open their doors in communities around the world. It speaks to our inherent human need to help others feel good about themselves (and our need to seek out joy and fulfillment). Personal trainers help people live longer, happier and more fulfilling lives. Personal trainers change lives for the better!

But before you take the "leap" into this new and exciting career path it's important to understand that there are several things to consider in order to do it right. Great personal trainers are not born ... they are made. It takes a significant amount of time and dedication to become a successful certified personal trainer who consistently provides a high standard of service and care. The path to a successful personal training career includes the following:

- Getting certified
- Practice. Practice. Practice.
- Understanding the business of personal training
- Creating a brand identity
- Opening up a successful business

Unfortunately, because of the popularity of this career path, personal trainers in the market range from being "dangerous" to real "life changers". There are several factors at play but the main reason is that a successful path for personal trainers has not been outlined (i.e. personal training business course).

Successful personal trainers are known for not only providing great services for their clients, they also use proven sales and marketing strategies to operate their business. If they were lucky they may have had a mentor or business partner to help them run the business. For everyone else, it meant doing their homework, doing the research, and trying different things until they got it right.

"The Business of Personal Training" was developed as a business guide for the fitness enthusiast looking to pursue a career as a personal trainer. In essence, a guide for the fitness entrepreneur. This book is designed to provide an easy-to-navigate path to becoming a well educated personal trainer with the business "savvy" to build a profitable business (without all of the pitfalls novice personal trainers may experience in the process).

Chapter 1:
Ready. Aim. Fire!

Congratulations on choosing to take the next step! That's GREAT! But now you're probably wondering ... "What do I do now?" and "How do I get started?".

Getting started on anything, regardless of what it is, isn't easy. It's even worse when there is no plan to follow or process to go through to ensure you are successful. It would be like baking a cake without a list of ingredients, proper measurements, or knowing what temperature to set the oven. You could get lucky but would most likely end up with a disaster on your hands.

To be successful in building a personal training business you need to do three (3) things:
1. Prepare your personal training business. (Ready.)
2. Market your personal training services. (Aim.)
3. Sell your personal training services. (Fire!)

Although the list is short, many people make the mistake of putting these steps in the wrong order.
1. Ready. Fire! Aim.
   You're prepared and you start selling before putting together effective strategies to make selling productive.

2. Aim. Fire! Ready.
   You've developed effective strategies and are successfully selling but are not prepared to deliver the services (i.e. no location to train).
3. Ready. Aim. Fire!
   You're prepared, have developed effective strategies to target sales and are successfully selling services.

A significant amount of time, effort and (potentially) money goes into building a personal training business. Using the wrong approach could waste valuable time and effort, result in unbearable frustration, and end up being very costly in the end.

READY - Prepare Your Personal Training Business
Running a personal training business is more than just helping another person exercise. It is a business with pros, cons and expectations that need to be well understood. The following are essential steps to follow as you prepare for the official launch of your personal training business:
1. Researching the industry
2. Getting certified
3. Establishing your personal training business

Making a career change is something that requires a good amount of thought before taking the big leap. Do your homework, discuss your thoughts and ideas with friends and family members that you trust and be well prepared before you take the next steps.

AIM - Market Your Personal Training Services
Once you've taken all of the appropriate steps to create an "official" personal training business, it's time to develop strategies to market the services you offer. Marketing is the process of communicating the value of your services to your potential customers. This can be done using a wide variety of media (i.e. face-to-face, in print, online).

Marketing your personal training business requires two crucial steps (ones that are often overlooked or completely forgotten):
1. Establishing your marketing budget
2. Identifying select marketing strategies to implement

FIRE - Sell Your Personal Training Services

Now that you've established the budget and identified specific marketing strategies to implement, it's time to start selling. Unfortunately, that may not be as easy as it sounds. "Selling" is something that doesn't typically come naturally for most personal trainers. Personal trainers choose this profession because helping others makes them feel good. Many of them say they would train clients for free because they love what they do so much. Regrettably, doing that wouldn't make for a successful (or profitable) business.

Selling doesn't come naturally for most people. When they are faced with asking for the sale, many stumble through and may not close a sale very often. Poor selling abilities will not help to build any business, whether it is selling personal training services or widgets.

Selling is a skill that needs to be learned, just like doing a push up or squat properly. It is a process that takes time and effort to learn, but will result in real sales when done right. Effective selling is a seven (7) step process (in order):
1. Prospecting
2. Pre-approach
3. Approach
4. Presentation and demonstration
5. Handling objections
6. Closing
7. Follow up

This final step is what can make or break a personal training business. You may be the most amazing personal trainer in the world but if you can't get people to pay for the services, your business won't survive.

Getting Started

As you can see the journey to starting a successful personal training business will take time, effort, and patience. The effort will be well worth it, if you are ready for the task, and this could be the last career you will ever need to pursue.

The first step begins with better understanding the fitness industry. The next chapter outlines a brief history of fitness, exercise and society's desire to become healthy and fit.

Chapter 2:
Getting to Know the Fitness Industry

Throughout history human beings have been engaging in physical activities to stay healthy and fit (whether they realized it or not). Prior to 1970, blue-collar workers held the majority of jobs in America. For this working class, manual labor was a normal part of everyday life. Pushing, pulling, lifting, carrying, running and a wide variety of physical tasks were part of a typical workday. Exercising (or participating in physical activity to develop or maintain fitness) wasn't necessary. In fact, back in 1960, only 24 percent of adults reported exercising routinely. It wasn't until the 1970s that Americans (primarily white-collar, middle class workers) began exercising on a regular basis. For this generation, work demands shifted from manual labor to office work requiring very little physical effort and the workday sitting idle at a desk.

Over the next two decades the idea of a "physical elite", an exclusive group of very active and fit human beings who exercised regularly (if not excessively), ate very clean and healthy, were self-aware and incredibly successful in their upper-middle income bracket jobs spurred the memberships of numerous country clubs and private social clubs across the country. It was, in essence, the idea of a "super race" committed to achieving the perfect body and mind through exercise and good nutrition.

As a result, participation in running groups and private clubs grew exponentially and at unprecedented rates. In addition, by 1987, a nationwide Gallup poll revealed 69 percent of Americans who reported exercising regularly.

Although commercial fitness centers have been around since the 1940s, the emergence of the modern fitness center was driven by cultural changes that shape the industry we see today. Attitudes towards health and wellness (or more accurately, obesity and associated preventable disease) fuel the continuous growth of the industry, affecting the habits and expectations of three generations of Americans and beyond.

Several cultural changes contributed to the fitness movement, including:
- The desire to be healthy
- The desire to "fit in"
- Corporate expectations and culture
- The changing roles of women
- The media

The Desire to Be Healthy
The idea of fitness (defined as "good health or physical condition, especially as the result of exercise and proper nutrition") came from a growing awareness of the deteriorating health and physical condition of most Americans. In the spring of 1968, Dr. Kenneth Cooper (widely recognized as "The Father of the Modern Fitness Movement") released his first best-selling book, "Aerobics". Selling more than 30 million copies to date, this ground breaking book, advocated a philosophy of disease prevention rather than conventional disease treatment. With a belief that "it is easier to maintain good health through proper exercise, diet and emotional balance than it is to regain it once it's lost", Dr. Cooper is credited with encouraging more individuals to exercise than any other person in history.

The release of this book could not have come at a better time. That same year the highest U.S. death rate for coronary heart disease was announced. This is significant because prior to the 1960s it was uncommon for people in their 50s and 60s to suffer from a heart attack. Also, 1968 marked the peak rate for deaths in U.S. history. Since then, the peak rate for deaths due to heart attack has declined by over 75 percent.

This new awareness brought forth the realization that (in the 1970s) this generation was the first in history who needed to intentionally seek out forms of exercise to keep fit. This new understanding got people motivated to get moving and get fit as exercise was viewed as preventive medicine. People became increasingly aware of the limitations of conventional medicine and physical activity was seen as a way to reduce stress and improve one's quality of life and longevity.

The Desire to "Fit In"
Generally, people don't like to do things that are only good for them. There needs to be motivating factors other than health. One example is "vanity". For some people, good health is not nearly as important as looking good and earning "physical elite" status. This led to negative attitudes towards looking obese or out of shape and, ultimately, motivated many to get off the couch and into their workout clothes and running shoes.

Corporation Expectations and Culture
Corporations first began helping employees with health-related issues (i.e. alcoholism and mental health) as early as the 1950s, it wasn't until the early 1980s that corporations started seriously looking at workplace wellness programs. Once reputable journals began reporting evidence on how corporations could reduce health care costs, reduce illness-related absences, and attract talented employees, employers quickly got on board.

Hundreds of firms established on-site fitness centers or set up contracts with local fitness clubs to subsidize employee memberships. These new employee benefits were used to promote healthful exercise for everyone, especially the upper-middle income bracket employees with higher company value. In fact, one study noted that 91 percent of executives exercised regularly by 1987.

As a result of the corporate wellness initiative, exercisers were among the "boomers" of the middle and professional classes. They were generally the more upscale, college-educated, white-collar professionals in the upper-middle income brackets.

The Changing Roles of Women
Women played an important role in expanding the fitness movement in the 1970s. Women turned to exercise for many reasons, initiated (to some degree) by the feminist movement. The feminist movement in America (from the 1960s to the 1980s) was concerned with gender inequality in laws and culture. Exercise featured an attitude of physical strength and fitness that translated to increased social empowerment for some women. A strong, toned body, built consciously to demonstrate control over life had replaced the slim, waif-like beauty of the 1960s.

Because of the increasing number of jobs in the workplace for women, more of them were deferring marriage and having children. By entering the work force they had more independence, wealth and money to spend on luxuries like a fitness club membership, to help them look better, feel better and relieve unwanted stress.

Finally, the addition of Title IX to the Civil Rights Act increased participation in sports and fitness exponentially. For example, the number of women in interscholastic sports grew from 300,000 to over 3.1 million in less than a decade (between 1970 and 1980).

The Media
Media has played a significant role in the fitness industry and how people perceive fitness as a whole. What we look like, how we exercise, and where we went to get fit became the next fashion accessory and status symbol that people revered. Trends came in the form of fitness attire, exercise workouts, home gym equipment, celebrity personal trainers, and reality weight loss television shows (like "The Biggest Loser").

Media has become the engine behind modern fitness and has spurred the growth of an industry that is now represented by 133,500 club locations around the world and a revenue of $71 billion in 2010 (2011 IHRSA Global Report).

The greatest contributor to these changing fitness trends has traditionally been the television. Although the internet has become an integral part of the day-to-day lives of the newest generation of trend mongers (Generation Z; born 1995-present), television is the gateway to evolving generations across the board ... changing their perceptions about fitness and exercise and dictating how their money is being spent (how they should look, how they should feel, how to accomplish these results). Table 2-1 outlines the milestones, from the 1930s to the present day, that have led to the fitness and exercise trends we see today.

Fitness in the 21st Century
Time to fast forward to the present day. In the twenty-first century, the driving force behind the fitness industry is obesity. Recent statistics reveal the reasons why. According to the Centers for Disease Control and Prevention (CDC), the majority of Americans are overweight and/or obese (2009-2010).
- 69.2% of adults 20 years and over are overweight, including obesity (BMI of 25 or higher)
- 35.9% of adults 20 years and over are obese (BMI of 30 or higher)
- 18.4% of adolescents age 12-19 years are obese
- 18.0% of children age 6-11 years who are obese
- 12.1% of children age 2-5 years who are obese

Overweight and obesity are both labels for weight ranges greater than what is generally considered healthy for a given height. These weight ranges have also been shown to increase the likelihood of certain diseases and other health problems.

Although body weight is affected by genetic and hormonal influences, obesity occurs when you take in more calories than you burn through exercise and normal daily activities. Your body stores these excess calories as fat. Obesity usually results from a combination of causes and contributing factors, but the two main reasons are:
- Inactivity
- Unhealthy diet and eating habits

As a response to the obesity epidemic, the fitness industry continues to grow at a steady pace. According to the International Health, Racquet and Sportsclub Association (IHRSA), the trade association serving the

health and fitness industry, as of January (2013):
- Number of US Health Clubs: 30,500
- Number of US Health Club Members: 51.3 million
- Total US Industry Revenues (2012): $21.8 billion

Unfortunately, this growth cannot supply the need as obesity rates also continue to rise. Although this may sound like bad news, this is a positive scenario for the individual looking to pursue a career in the fitness industry as a personal trainer or fitness professional.

In the following chapters you will learn about the personal training profession, how to get started and how to build a successful business helping people change their lives through fitness and exercise.

Table 2-1

Evolution of Modern Fitness (as portrayed by the media)

1938	**Superman** • "Faster than a speeding bullet! More powerful than a locomotive! Able to leap tall buildings at a single bound!" • This iconic superhero gave the world a vision of what the "perfect" male specimen would look like. Men aspired to be him and women longed to be his Lois Lane!
1940	**Vic Tanny** • "Take it off. Build it up. Make it firm." • Victor (Vic) Tanny was a pioneer of health clubs as we know them today.
1941	**Charles Atlas** • Featured in pint advertisements predominantly found in comic books. • Developed the Dynamic Tension system of physical exercises. • "Hey skinny! Yer ribs are showing!" • "Nobody picks on a strong man."
1956	**Jack LaLanne** • "The Godfather of Fitness" • At the age of 65, he towed 65 boats filled with 6,500 pounds while handcuffed and shackled near Tokyo, Japan.
1976	**Rocky (Sylvester Stallone)** • A small-time boxer gets a rare chance to fight the heavyweight champion in a bout in which he strives to go the distance for his self-respect. • This movie reminded us all what it meant to be the "underdog". • "Gonna Fly Now", the theme song from the movie, is a favorite on many motivational iTunes playlists.
1977	**Pumping Iron** • In this half fact, half fiction, part-scripted, part-documentary film, five-time champion, Arnold Schwarzenegger defends his Mr. Olympia title against Serge Nubret and Lou Ferrigno. • This movie led to the acting careers of both Arnold ("Conan the Barbarian" and "The Terminator") and Lou Ferrigno ("The Incredible Hulk").

Table 2-1 (cont'd)

Evolution of Modern Fitness (as portrayed by the media)

1977	**Jim Fixx** • Author of the "Complete Book of Running". • Credited for popularizing the sport of running, starting America's fitness revolution, and demonstrating of the health benefits of regular jogging. **Jazzercise** • "Let the music move you." • "Push your body. Find your beat. Jazzercise." • On the 2011 Entrepreneur Franchise 500 list, Jazzercise ranks as the #1 fitness franchise (#17 in the complete franchise list).
1982	**Jane Fonda Workout** • Jane Fonda made leotards, spandex, leg warmers, head bands, and wrist bands the newest fashion trend. • "No pain, no gain." • "Feel the burn." **Let's Get Physical (Olivia Newton-John)** • "Let's Get Physical" was the first music video showcasing physical fitness and exercise. • "Let me hear your body talk." • "I want to get animal, animal."
1985	**Perfect (John Travolta and Jamie Lee Curtis)** • A film based on a series of articles appearing in Rolling Stone magazine in the late 1970s, chronicling the popularity of LA fitness health clubs with the single crowd.
1987	**Hans & Franz (Saturday Night Live)** • "I am Hans." ... "Und I am Franz." • "Und ve just vant to pump ... (clap) ... YOU UP!" • "Poor little girlie man alone in his girlie house!" **The Gazelle (Tony Little)** • Successfully introduces one of the first infomercials for home fitness equipment. • "Conceive, believe, and achieve." • "You can do it!"
1988	Sweatin' to the Oldies (Richard Simmons) • "Dance Your Pants Off" • "Blast Off the Pounds" • "Never Say Diet"

Table 2-1 (cont'd)
Evolution of Modern Fitness (as portrayed by the media)

1989	**Tae Bo (Billy Blanks)** • "Hollywood's Healthy Alternative to Heroin." • "An amazing blend of tae kwon do, boxing, aerobics, and dance into one complete system."
1990	**Body for Life (Bill Phillips)** • Body for Life is a 12-week nutrition and exercise program. • "The true measure of success is revealed only by looking at the obstacles that an individual had to overcome to achieve their goals." **Body by Jake (Jake Steinfeld)** • "There is only one BODY BY JAKE!" • "Stick to the fight when you are hardest hit, it's when things seem worst that you must not quit!" • "Don't quit on you!"
1991	**Thighmaster (Suzanne Somers)** • Suzanne Somers started the "Somersizing" phenomenon. • "It's easy to squeeze, squeeze your way to shapely hips and thighs." • "We may not have been born with great legs but now we can look like we were." **Shape Your Body Workout (Cindy Crawford)** • Also known as the "supermodel workout". • This "toning" video is an example of what NOT to do in a workout (because you could really get hurt). **Curves for Women** • A fitness franchise targeted to the needs of women, Curves opened 7,000 locations in under a decade (it took McDonald's and Subway more than 25 years). • "No makeup, no men, and no mirrors."
1993	**Susan Powter** • "Stop the Insanity!" • "The Lenny Bruce of Wellness" (by Shape Magazine) • She described herself to Curve magazine as a "radical feminist lesbian woman."
1996	**G.I. Jane (Demi Moore)** • A female Senator succeeds in enrolling a woman into Combined Reconnaissance Team training where everyone expects her to fail. • Chin ups, pull ups and one-arm push ups soon became fitness goals for more women and arm workouts became more popular.

Table 2-1 (cont'd)

Evolution of Modern Fitness (as portrayed by the media)

1997	**Total Gym (Chuck Norris & Christie Brinkley)** • "Once you try it, you'll be hooked for life." • "Lean, mean exercise machine"
1999	**Fight Club (Brad Pitt & Edward Norton)** • An insomniac office worker crosses paths with a devil-may-care soap maker and they form an underground fight club that evolves into something much more ... • This movie inspired websites and workouts specifically geared towards Brad Pitt's physique (The "Fight Club Workout").
2001	**Zumba (Alberto Perez)** • "Ditch the Workout. Join the Party" • "When the music starts pumping, people forget they're exercising. And that just may be the secret to Zumba's success."
2004	**Biggest Loser (Bob Harper and Jillian Michaels)** • "You need to find your OWN purpose. I cannot BUILD desire." • "Believe in yourself, trust the process, change forever." • "I know it hurts but I'm saving your life right now." **P90X (Tony Horton)** • "Extreme Home Fitness" using the advanced science of "Muscle Confusion" • "Bring it!" • "I hate it ... but I LOVE IT!"
2006	**Wii Fit (Nintendo)** • The first commercial retail "active gaming" system available • Wii Fit combines fitness with fun and is designed for everyone, young and old. • "How will it move you?"
2009	**The Shake Weight** • "Get strong, sexy, sculpted arms and shoulders." • "Get toned, defined, and stronger ... fast!" **Insanity Workout (Shaun T.)** • This Beachbody workout "improves fitness in 60 days through strenuous stamina training". • "The Insanity Workout might just be the hardest fitness program ever put on DVD."

Table 2-1 (cont'd)
Evolution of Modern Fitness (as portrayed by the media)

2010	***Xbox Kinect (Microsoft)*** • "Games are more amazing when you are the controller." • "You already know how to play. All you have to do now is get off the couch."
2012	***Brazil Butt Lift (Leandro Carvahlo)*** • "Gives you that higher, tighter, rounder butt in just 60 days." • "Works the TRIANGLE which includes the three main muscles of the buttocks: medius, minimus and the gluteus maximus."
2013	***Spartacus Workout (Men's Health and Starz)*** • Based on the Starz original series, Men's Health created the original Spartacus Workout in 2011. Because of overwhelming popularity, the sequel to the workout was produced in a workout DVD set. • "It will make you sweat. It will make your muscles burn. And it will kick your butt."

Chapter 3:
What is Personal Training?

Personal trainers are fitness experts who help clients attain greater awareness and understanding in the areas of fitness and health. Personal trainers also provide clients with motivation and challenges (physical and emotional) as they work towards improving their physical fitness through exercise. In a nutshell, personal trainers provide valuable information to a client. They are a fitness "coach" or "mentor" that helps to guide a client to becoming the best physical being they can be.

Personal training, as the collection of services offered to clients, includes the following:
- Motivating clients by setting goals and providing consistent feedback
- Identifying a client's strengths and weaknesses
- Providing advice on cardiovascular exercise, resistance exercise, stretching exercises, nutrition and general health matters
- Guiding clients on the proper exercise technique
- Developing exercise programs to help clients improve their fitness and overall health
- Evaluating client progress, modifying existing programs and keeping them on track to reaching their personal fitness goals
- Being there every step of the way ... and holding clients accountable to the work they need to complete

Personal training is also ... PERSONAL! Each client is different (strengths, weaknesses, needs, goals and expectations). No two people are alike and the same holds true for a physical fitness program. An effective fitness program is ever changing and evolving to match the needs of the client as they change over time.

Why Choose a Career as a Personal Trainer?
Some personal trainers choose this profession based on personal reasons (i.e. to help others, to be a role model, to be able to wear workout clothes all day long). Unfortunately, these types of reasons are not the right kind when it comes to making important business decisions. Facts and reliable evidence is necessary to ensure you are making sound decisions. Luckily, there are several compelling reasons why a personal training career is one to strongly consider.

1. The Fitness Industry is Growing
   According to the Bureau of Labor Statistics employment of fitness instructors and personal trainers will increase by 24% between 2010 to 2020. The demand for "proactive" health and fitness solutions is on the rise and certified personal trainers will have a wide variety of opportunities moving forward.

2. Diversity of Workplace
   Personal trainers can provide their services in a wide variety of locations. As long as the environment is safe and provides adequate space and the proper equipment, a personal trainer can do their job. Common locations for personal training include:
   - Fitness club or recreation facility
   - Specialty studio or wellness facility
   - Sports performance training facility
   - Medical facility or hospital
   - Corporate head office
   - In home training

3. Diversity of Client Population
   To be honest, the client population for personal training pretty well includes those who have two feet and a heartbeat. To be more specific I would include clients who are at least old enough

to walk, can communicate effectively and have a maturity to comply with the program. The various client populations to service encompass a broad spectrum including:
- Pre/Post Natal Fitness
- Senior Fitness
- Children's/Youth Fitness
- Chronic Disease & Disabilities
- Rehabilitation

Not all personal trainers choose a specialty in their education and certification. However, specialized training gives a personal trainer a way to differentiate themselves from others where they can focus their expertise and create a higher value of service.

3. Flexible Hours

   Personal training can happen at any time during the day (365, 24/7). In the end, personal training sessions are at the discretion of the personal trainer and the client (at a time agreed upon between the two parties). Because of the wide variety of locations a personal trainer can offer services the schedule is wide open. For example, personal training can be accommodated at a fitness club in the morning, at a corporate head office in the afternoon and at a client's home in the evening.

4. Ongoing Education and Training

   The fitness industry is fairly new and has a lot of opportunity for growth and expansion. With the growing need for proactive health care solutions there is also growing interest to learn more and to evolve the industry in a positive way. With that being said, new research findings are being published on a regular basis, new training techniques are being introduced to the market and new tools and technologies are constantly being introduced that are designed to make it easier to get physical results in a safe and effective way.

   In order to stay competitive in a career field like personal training it is imperative to stay ahead of the pack and truly become a "fitness expert". There are a wide variety of fitness education and certification providers with varying areas of expertise. There are also opportunities to learn from other personal trainers and fitness experts at their studios, clinics, research labs and training facilities. Regardless, successful personal trainers should be "eternal students" as it is highly unlikely that there will ever be an end to the variety of tools that can be included in their personal training tool box.

Personal training is a career with a long "shelf life". Not only does it offer many positive incentives as a function of the job itself, it also has a bright future. Much like the food and beverage industry, which relies on the guarantee that people will always need to eat, the fitness industry relies on the guarantee that people will want to be healthy and live a long and prosperous life.

The next chapter looks closely at the reasons why people seek out personal trainers and their importance in a time where the majority of the population needs help getting fit and healthy.

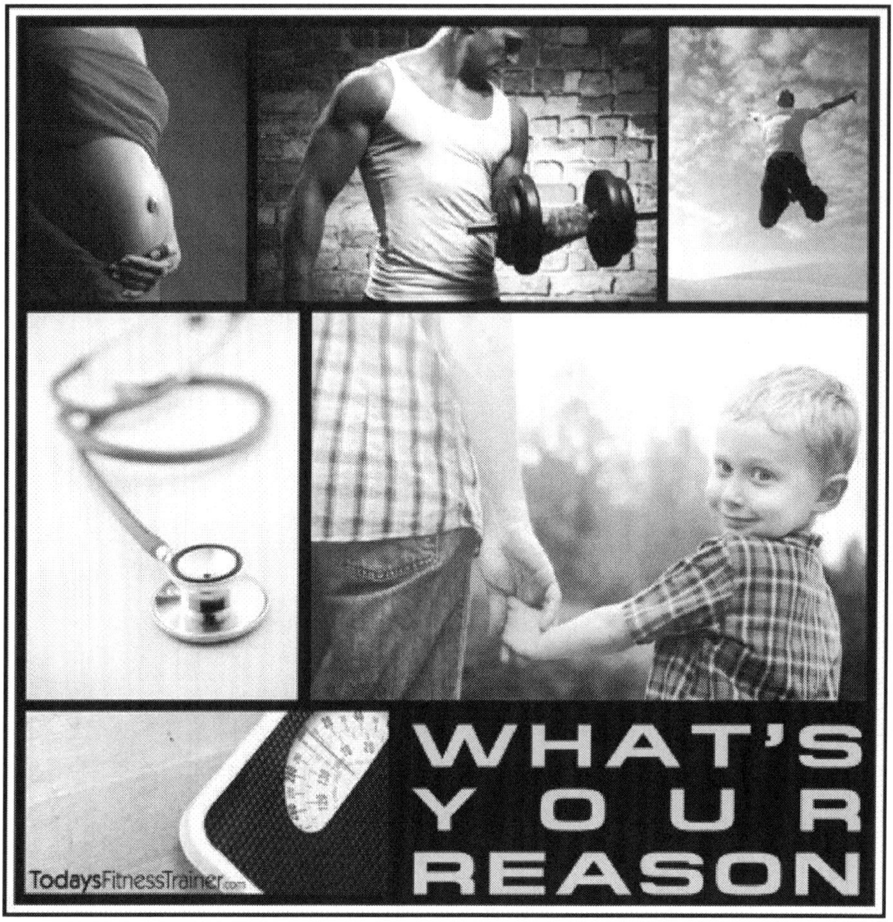
WHAT'S
YOUR
REASON
TodaysFitnessTrainer.com

Chapter 4:
Reasons Why People Hire a Personal Trainer

There are currently over 316 million people living in America, most striving to live a long and healthy life. According to the 2008 Physical Activity Guidelines for Americans, engaging in 150 minutes of moderate intensity physical activity per week has been proven to promote good overall health. Sadly, only 15 percent of the population are members of a fitness club (some not even using it regularly), leaving the majority of the population in need of help getting off the couch and getting healthy!

Personal trainers shoulder the responsibility of helping people overcome various obstacles that get in between them and their fitness goal. Considering recent statistics, that leaves an abundance of opportnity to help people change their lives!

Everybody is different but there is a common theme to why people pay for personal training services. Below is a list of common reasons why people consider hiring a personal trainer:
- They are new to exercise (or exercise has been recommended by a physician).
- They need added motivation to exercise.
- They have questions about exercise (and may be afraid to do it on their own).
- They've hit a "plateau" in their progress.

- They're "bored" with their current workout routine.
- They are training for a sport (or upcoming event).
- They're having (or recently had) a baby.
- They're recovering from an injury (and exercise has been recommended by their physical therapist/rehabilitation specialist).
- They're looking to get faster results.
- They are considering a career as a personal trainer.

New to Exercise
For the 85% of people in the country who are not members of a fitness club, it can be a very intimidating place. Top reasons why people don't exercise or join a club include:
- They don't like exercise.
- They don't know how to exercise.
- They aren't motivated to exercise.
- They can't commit to an exercise routine.
- They don't have time.

A certified personal trainer, first and foremost, provides education and guidance. Knowledge is power and, in a fitness setting, it is also a source of confidence and motivation. By providing information in a supportive environment, your client can learn a lot about the services you offer as his/her trainer, about exercise in general, and how to motivate themselves to continue down the path of success.

Secondly, a personal trainer is a coach and part of a client's support team. Because a client is accountable to their support team there are no excuses. The fact that they've paid for services, makes them responsible for showing up and getting the work done. In essence, you provide your client with a reason to get out the front door to get to the gym. They rely on the fact that you will be supportive in their workouts to ensure they are safe and that they get the most out of each workout.

Motivation
Motivation (by definition) is generally a desire or willingness of someone to do something. Motivation can be either "intrinsic" (where motivation comes from enjoyment from doing the task itself, without the need for outside factors) or "extrinsic" (where motivation comes

from the knowledge that performing an activity will be rewarded with an outcome). In other words, someone who is intrinsically motivated does an activity because it makes them feel good. Someone who is extrinsically motivated is expecting a reward for doing something (i.e. money, recognition, a reason to buy new clothes). No matter what the task (from doing the actual exercise to simply getting out the front door and to the gym), if there isn't enough reason to do it ... a person won't even get started.

Personal trainers are in the business of motivation! They are the masters when it comes to getting people motivated to exercise ... and to keep doing it! Not only do they give a client a reason to simply get out the front door and to the gym, they also provide feedback and emotional support to help clients get the most out of each exercise and every workout.

Education
If you look on the internet there are a million different websites that provide information about fitness and exercise. With so much information available (good or bad) it can be confusing for anyone trying to figure out what's right for their body when they have a specific physical goal in mind. Certified personal trainers are sought out because they are educated by organizations that are the authorities in fitness. In addition, they are required to maintain a level of knowledge in their field. Therefore, personal trainers are the best people to ask when a client isn't sure about the latest fad they read in Men's Health or Shape or if they need good advice about certain exercises and how to perform them correctly. Clients can learn a lot from each session with a personal trainer that can produce significant results over time.

Hit a "Plateau"
Regardless of whether someone is new to exercise or Michael Phelps chasing his 22nd Olympic medal, the body is destined to experience plateaus (no improvement in exercise performance). In order for the body to change, it needs to be exposed to challenges that force it to make changes. In other words, the body needs to be pushed out of its "comfort zone" in order to change. Unfortunately, human beings are creatures of habit and gravitate to actions that make them feel safe,

competent and confident.

Certified personal trainers are walking "fitness encyclopedias". The biggest difference between a certified personal trainer and someone who reads a lot about fitness is ... experience! It is the difference between someone reading a Betty Crocker cookbook at Barnes and Noble and the Executive Chef of an award winning restaurant trained at the Culinary Institute of America. Personal trainers work with several clients and translate their knowledge into tangible results each and every day. They have experience knowing what works, what doesn't and how to create programs that match the needs of a wide variety of people.

Current Workout Routine is "Boring"
Human beings are creatures of habit. They follow routines in much of what they do everyday (i.e. foods they eat, the route they take to work, the shows they watch on TV), including their workout routine. Over time, if the routine doesn't change, boredom is inevitable. Because the workouts are boring:
- The workouts aren't enjoyable.
- People aren't motivated to work as hard.
- People aren't motivated to visit the gym as often.
- People won't get the expected results.

Certified personal trainers can help a client "spice up" their workouts with new exercises, new training techniques and complete programs to give them new ways to challenge themselves. A personal trainer can also assess overall fitness (muscular strength, muscular endurance, cardiovascular endurance/capacity, flexibility, etc.), identify strengths and weaknesses, develop a customized workout program based on specific goals, and take the client through the workouts to ensure proper form and technique for positive results.

Training for a Sport (or upcoming event)
Whether someone is learning a brand new activity or sport, is a weekend warrior or competes at a high level in their chosen sport an effective fitness and exercise program can greatly benefit their overall performance. Millimeters and milliseconds can be the difference between winning and losing.

The ability to perform during a sporting event relies on how the body functions (i.e. strength, endurance, reaction time, speed, flexibility, etc.) and the structure of the body (i.e. muscles, bones, ligaments, tendons, heart, lungs, etc.). Practices, drills, and competitions help improve athletic ability but they won't necessarily change the structure of the body. On the flip side, changing the structure of the body can significantly improve athletic ability.

Personal trainers with experience in sport-specific training can develop workout programs that address the needs of a specific sport. Sport-specific programs are designed to enhance athletic performance while decreasing the chance of injury. Well designed programs take into account the need for rest and recovery, an athlete's strengths and weaknesses (as it relates to the sport) and their training schedule and competition deadlines.

Having (or recently had) a Baby
An expecting mother experiences physical, social and emotional changes during and after pregnancy. Being prepared and educated can help them to accept their changing body and give them the right tools to deal with their emotions. Labor is a very physically demanding experience that requires a great deal of physical stamina, strength and awareness. A personal trainer experienced in pre-natal fitness can be a valuable addition to a woman's pre-natal plans if she is looking:
- To start an exercise program to improve overall health.
- To stay consistently active during the pregnancy.
- To make modifications to an existing workout program (used before the pregnancy began) to ensure safety during exercise.
- To effectively exercise specific muscles needed for labor.
- For support and feedback as her body goes through major changes (ie. motivation, self-confidence and support).

In several studies women who exercised regularly after the birth of their baby reported more rapid physical and emotional recovery than those who did not. A personal trainer with post-natal fitness experience can be extremely helpful in getting women back to their "pre-baby" body shape and weight. Post-natal programs, supervised by a personal trainer, can:

- Accommodate for the limited amount of time a mother with an infant may have to exercise.
- Outline suitable exercises and modify them as the body returns back to its pre-pregnancy state (ie. hormonal changes).
- Address the change in energy levels and physical abilities of a mother with an infant.

Recovery from Injury
Regardless of how an injury happens it can have a major effect on a person's daily life. The process of letting the body heal and getting it back to the level of fitness prior to the injury can be a daunting task.

Common reasons why people who are injured avoid exercising (even though it is beneficial to their rehabilitation) include:
- Fear that the injury could get worse.
- Fear that they could sustain another injury.
- Not knowing how to manage the pain associated with the injury.

A personal trainer can be a great addition to any rehabilitation program. Personal trainers experienced in injury rehabilitation not only provide exercise programs designed to help rebuild the strength and flexibility of the affected area, these exercise programs can also strengthen the supporting structures to help a client gain confidence as they learn to function in their day to day lives. With careful exercise selection and effective program development a client can regain strength and stability, while reducing and alleviating tightness and pain.

Looking for Faster Results
Changing the physical make-up of the human body is a science. Changing the body is kind of like baking a cake. You need the right combination of ingredients (in the right amounts), the oven needs to be set at the right temperature and the alarm needs to be set to the appropriate time. To change the body a person needs a program with the right combination of exercises, the right level of intensity for each workout, adequate rest and recovery time in between workouts and a deadline to reach. Personal trainers are experts at juggling all of these elements to help a client achieve their end goal.

A fitness and exercise "recipe book" is especially important for an inexperienced exerciser who can benefit from learning exercise basics, safe exercise practices and who needs help staying on a regularly scheduled program. A seasoned exerciser can also benefit from the education, program structure and consistent schedule. A personal trainer can provide the knowledge, experience and third-person perspective needed for a client to start seeing measurable results. The more fit a person is, the more challenging it can be to see changes in the body and the more specific a fitness program needs to be.

Considering a Career as a Personal Trainer
It isn't uncommon for fitness enthusiasts to consider a career as a personal trainer. If they work with a personal trainer, the likelihood is even higher because they know how the professional can impact lives. One of the best ways for them to learn is by spending time with different personal trainers. If they have never worked with a personal trainer, having the perspective of a client can be helpful in better understanding the nature of the work, what styles of training they like and don't like, what type of environment they would like to work in (i.e. fitness club, small studio, in-home, corporate office, school, etc.) and the business side of one-on-one or group personal training.

Having one or more mentors is invaluable as they seek a new and exciting career in fitness. By hiring a personal trainer they effectively establish good relationships with peers, versus creating competition in a very competitive market. This is a smart investment in their personal trainer education and certification.

In summary, if a person has two feet, a heartbeat and a fitness or exercise goal, they can benefit from the services of a personal trainer. The challenge is getting the right message to a targeted audience. Future chapters will discuss focused strategies on branding, marketing and sales.

Chapter 5:
7 Habits of Highly Effective Personal Trainers

According to the 2011 IBISWorld Personal Trainer Market Research Report, there are over 230,000 personal trainers in the U.S. employed by over 50,000 businesses. Personal training generates over $7 billion in revenue each year. But much like all other businesses, the "80-20 Rule" applies (80 percent of the business is driven by 20 percent of the population). Being an exceptional personal trainer (or any career one may choose) doesn't happen by accident. Mastering a skill and becoming a market leader requires hard work and a concrete plan. Vince Lombardi, best known as the head coach of the Green Bay Packers in the 1960s, said it best:

"Leaders aren't born they are made. And they are made just like anything else, through hard work. And that's the price we'll have to pay to achieve that goal, or any goal."

Effective personal trainers employ several habits that make them the 20 percent of the market making 80 percent of the money. Exceptional personal trainers:
- Approach personal training as a business (while still maintaining a true passion for what they do).
- Are goal-oriented and proactive.
- Manage their time effectively.

- Understand the importance of client satisfaction and care.
- Make education and learning a priority.
- Create a strong brand for their business.
- Create a high value of worth for their services.

Personal Training as a Business
Most personal trainers start their career because they have a passion for helping people achieve their physical fitness goals. Unfortunately, passion and enjoyment in one's job doesn't guarantee a successful, money making business. Only a small percentage of personal trainers have the knowledge or experience in building and maintaining a successful entrepreneurial business.

Any successful business, whether it's a small "Mom and Pop" outfit or a globally recognized corporation, needs a well thought out plan and strategies to achieve success. This includes the following components:
1. Business plan (What is the business? What makes it "special"? How does it fulfill a need in the market space? How will it overcome inherent challenges in the market space? What differentiates it from competitors? How will you know it is successful?)
2. Business operations and finances (start up costs, revenue projections, accounting, legal, etc.)
3. Sales and marketing strategies (web, social media and print)

These three components are crucial to making a personal training business a success. The responsibilities of running a business are crucial to ensuring:
- Existing clients are satisfied (and continue to purchase services).
- The business continues to grow (maximizing clients and revenue potential).
- Decreasing unnecessary costs and expenses.
- Freedom to enjoy time away from the business (without putting the business in jeopardy).

Setting Goals (and making them happen)
Personal trainers understand the human body and how to help clients change their bodies to meet their physical fitness goals. Setting goals in business can be challenging if a personal trainer doesn't feel comfortable

or knowledgeable about their business. Regardless, setting short-term and long-term goals for the business is critical to overall success. The goals outlined for the business set the path, checkpoints and journey for the business to ensure it's staying on track over time.

Goals for the business may include:
- Number of clients under contract
- Amount of revenue generated
- Timeline to open first studio location
- Timeline to open additional studio locations
- Strategic partnerships to grow/expand the business
- Timeline to sell the business (retirement)

Goals should be specific, measurable, attainable, realistic and on a timeline (S.M.A.R.T. Principle).

Time Management
A personal trainer running a successful business must juggle the time dedicated to training clients and running the business. Time management is a very important part of creating a successful personal training business because it directly effects the delivery of services to a client and their overall satisfaction. Personal training, as a service, is very "hands on" and is built on the relationship between the personal trainer and client (i.e. trust and mutual respect). Things to avoid include:
- Showing up late to a personal training appointment
- Missing a personal training appointment (i.e. scheduling the wrong day)
- Canceling a personal training appointment

Suggested strategies to improve time management include:
- Effective appointment scheduling (day planner, online calendar, scheduling software program)
- Set a standard working schedule (i.e. Monday to Friday, 8:00am to 5:00pm)
- Allocating time each day for business administration

Human beings are creatures of habit. By creating a standard schedule a personal trainer can maintain balance between their work and personal obligations without the added stress. The business relies on the health and wellness of the personal trainer. If they are over-stressed or unable to train clients, the business will fail.

Client Satisfaction and Care
The overall goal of a personal training business is to provide exceptional service and care for paying clients. When clients are happy and satisfied with their results they are more likely to:
- Continue with their personal training.
- Refer friends and family.
- Provide testimonials for marketing purposes.

This area of the business requires the majority of a personal trainer's attention. This requires the development of effective training programs, the delivery of good personal training experiences, good communication with all clients and effective strategies to promote ongoing sales.

Making Continuing Education a Priority
Fitness is still considered a "young" and evolving industry. There are constantly new ideas, concepts and innovative ways being introduced to the market to help people improve their bodies and live healthier and better quality lives. It is important for personal trainers to maintain awareness of what's new and what can help them improve their business. Continuing education courses and workshops:
- Provide personal trainers with ways to differentiate themselves from their competitors.
- Keep personal trainers up to date with what is new and what other personal trainers may be adding to their service offering.
- Provide personal trainers with new and innovative tools to help them run their businesses better.
- Make personal training more fun and exciting!

The more effective, efficient and innovative a personal trainer can be … the more value they can bring to their existing and future clients.

Creating a "Brand" for the Business
A brand is a what differentiates one personal trainer's services from others in the market. The goal of developing an effective personal

training brand is to accentuate the qualities or characteristics of a personal trainer's services that make them special or unique. A brand is therefore one of the most valuable elements in marketing a personal trainer's service offering.

Elements of an effective brand include:
- Business logo
- Business slogans and tag lines
- Consistent written content (marketing materials, website)
- Proprietary programs and services (branded programs, written publications, YouTube channel, DVDs, etc.)
- Personal trainer's appearance/attire (design and style, business logos)
- Personal trainer's communication style
- Personal trainer's physical gestures and actions

The personal trainer essentially becomes the brand. What they say, how they look and what they do all reflect the expectation of experience that they are trying to sell ... their one-on-one services with each personal training client.

Creating a High Value of Worth for Personal Training
Personal training is not a commodity that has a set value based on market needs and demand. For example, a one gallon jug of milk costs approximately three dollars in the U.S. and the price is consistent in most cities. Milk is essentially the same no matter where you buy it. Personal training, on the other hand, can range from ten dollars to upwards of one thousand dollars an hour (i.e. celebrity personal trainers). According to the IDEA Health and Fitness Association, a typical session rate ranges from fifty to sixty dollars per hour (taking into account all levels of personal trainers in the market). Keep in mind that, in today's consumer market, people will pay more for services if they believe they are worth it.

Exceptional personal trainers create a high value for their services by effectively incorporating all of the strategies outlined in this series (habits 1 through 6). It is important to consider the following when determining the value of your services:

- Don't undervalue your services.
- Don't overvalue your services.
- Be confident in your ability to deliver services that dictate the price.

By confidently selling your personal training services at a higher value you end up working "smarter" and not "harder". You are providing a high quality of service without having to provide a large quantity. This way you end up working less, making more money and maintaining a balance between your career and your personal life.

The only thing stopping an average personal trainer from being one of the most successful personal trainers in business is commitment to an effective business plan and dedication to reaching their business goals. In future chapters, details on the business side and development of effective strategies is further discussed.

Chapter 6:
Health Care Reform and the Fitness Industry

On March 23, 2010, President Obama signed the Patient Protection and Affordable Care Act (PPACA) in an effort to set the health of our nation in a different direction ... one focused on prevention and proactive care. Primary areas of focus (in general terms) include:
- Increasing access to affordable care
- Improving quality and lowering costs
- Preventing disease and illness

What started out as a great idea and initiative became official on June 28, 2012, when the Supreme Court ruled that the health care law wasconstitutional.

But what does that really mean for the future of the fitness industry? What effect does it have on industry growth? In what ways will it contribute to new opportunities in business and career development?

The fitness industry is dedicated to preventing disease and improving quality of life through exercise and physical activity. These initiatives are aligned with the goals of the PPACA. The challenge over the next few years will be to "bridge the gap" between policy and implementation in an effort to get Americans more proactive with their health to ensure they have a better quality of life.

The Prevention and Public Health Fund
The Affordable Care Act's Prevention and Public Health Fund is designed to expand and sustain the necessary capacity to prevent disease, detect it early, manage conditions before they become severe, and provide states and communities the resources they need to promote healthy living. The $10 billion fund (originally $15 billion), allocated over ten years, will be distributed to states and communities to boost prevention and public health efforts, improve health, enhance health care quality and foster the next generation of primary health professionals. The funds are dedicated to expanding on four critical priorities:
- Community prevention (including obesity prevention and fitness)
- Clinical prevention (including employer wellness programs)
- Public Health infrastructure and training
- Research and tracking

The government has invested in a long term plan dedicated to the proactive health and wellness of Americans. The goal of this initiative is to get the country statistically healthier by 2020. This works in conjunction with the Healthy People 2020 campaign spearheaded by the Office of Disease Prevention and Health Promotion (ODPHP).

Bridging the Gap Between Health Care and the Fitness Industry
Research proves that exercise has a role in the treatment and prevention of over 40 chronic diseases, including diabetes, heart disease, obesity and hypertension. If started early enough, exercise and physical activity are powerful tools that can reverse the effects of these conditions and can provide the foundation for a life free of these diseases. Regular exercise has been recognized as a "magic bullet" as the country takes aggressive steps towards reversing the effects of nationwide obesity over the next ten years.

The first of these initiatives starts with the PPACA. The PPACA has outlined policies designed to motivate Americans to be more proactive about their physical health (and the health of others). The following are three policies outlined in the Act:
1. Most U.S. Citizens and legal residents must have health insurance.
2. Employers must offer health insurance coverage to their employees (employers with 50+ full-time employees).

3. Grants are available for small businesses to establish wellness programs (up to $50,000 over three years).

By producing policies that direct all Americans in the same preventive direction, the goal is to develop healthy habits over time for the next generation to follow and pass on. Let's take a closer look at the policies listed above and what that means to the fitness industry.

Mandatory Health Insurance for U.S. Citizens

Most U.S. citizens and legal residents will be required to have health insurance. In an effort to get 94% of the population covered by some form of health care, "health insurance exchanges" were developed to offer insurance options for individuals who did not have access to an employer-sponsored insurance or a public plan (ie. Medicare or Medicaid). The bad news (for those not covered by their employer or Medicare/Medicaid) may be that everyone is now required to have health insurance coverage. The good news (for the rest of us) is insurance companies are being pressured to keep pricing consistent and competitive for standardized packages.

How would this affect the fitness industry?
1. People will be motivated to find ways to lower their insurance premiums
2. People will want to get the most out of their insurance coverage (now that they pay for it)

The healthier you are, the lower your insurance premiums. If you are unhealthy and "at risk" for preventable disease, your insurance premiums sky rocket. As people become more educated about these cost savings that are a direct result of being more healthy and fit they are more likely to seek out fitness services and support (i.e. fitness club membership, personal training). In the end, the immediate cost of these services is worth the long term cost savings from lower insurance premiums.

In today's "value" economy, people are looking to get the most out of their health insurance. Some health insurance plans provide reimbursements for fitness club memberships, program fees, home fitness equipment and personal training (check with your insurance provider to see what is covered/reimbursed through their plans).

Mandatory Health Insurance Provided by Employers (50+ full time employees)

According to the Kaiser Family Foundation Employer Health Benefits 2011 Annual Survey, employers are the principle source of health insurance for over 150 million non-elderly workers in America. With over 230 million employed workers in the U.S. (July 2011) that would mean over 80 million are not covered by an employer sponsored insurance plan. The changes to the PPACA are designed to change this trend.

With many employer sponsored insurance plans, the employer and employee split the cost of the monthly premiums. Both parties are looking to get the cost of the insurance premiums down and get the most value for what they are paying for.

Grants for Employee Wellness Programs (small businesses)

Small businesses (less than 100 employees that work 25+ hours/week) can take advantage of grant funding to establish a workplace wellness program. A budget of $200 million has been set aside in support of this program (available until 2015). To qualify for the grant the workplace wellness program must include four components:
- Initiatives that include health education, preventive screenings and health risk assessments.
- Mechanisms to maximize employee participation and engagement.
- Initiatives to change unhealthy behaviors and lifestyle choices, including counseling, seminars, online programs and self-help materials.
- Supportive environment efforts that include workplace policies to encourage healthy lifestyles, healthy eating, increased physical activity and improved mental health.

This initiative opens the door to opportunities for personal trainers to offer onsite services and to establish workplace wellness programs that involve fitness and exercise. As the area of corporate wellness grows the job opportunities will also expand. The infusion of funds from this initiative will also drive a higher demand in the upcoming years.

The recognition of the Patient Protection and Affordable Care Act by the Senate is a huge step in securing resources for a healthier tomorrow. With the establishment of the PPACA, fitness professionals have an exciting opportunity to do more with their knowledge and skills ... but only if they choose to take action.

Chapter 7:
Personal Trainer = Fitness Entrepreneur

The life of a typical personal trainer is very hectic and incredibly unpredictable! Unlike a person who works in a sales or management role in a fitness club, one with a 9 to 5 job, set roles and responsibilities and job security, a personal trainer traditionally works in a contract role with limited guarantees. In order to be successful in their career (and make enough money to make it worthwhile), most personal trainers have to become "fitness entrepreneurs". Unfortunately, most have little to no experience running a business (let alone a successful one)!

Being a personal trainer is a "feel good" career. The majority of personal trainers truly love what they do and have a passion for helping people. It's not uncommon to hear someone say they would do it for "free", if they didn't have to make a living. They choose this career in spite of the following conditions:
- Training clients at all hours of the day (very early morning to very late at night).
- Teaching group classes for multiple fitness clubs and studios (as an independent contractor).
- Lack of health insurance or work benefits (most personal trainers are independent contractors and do not qualify for benefits or incentives).

Unfortunately, most personal trainers are underpaid and many struggle to survive on their current salary (when employed by a fitness center or workout gym). According to the Bureau of Labor Statistics (a division of the United States Department of Labor), 251,400 fitness trainers and instructors in 2010 made an average of $31,090 (below the national average of $33,840). Of these, the majority worked for fitness and recreation sports centers (61%) and very few were self-employed (8%). Because of the hectic work conditions it is unrealistic for them to take on a second job to make ends meet.

Personal trainers already have many of the traits that make up a successful entrepreneur. According to Dr. Michael Woodward, CEC certified executive coach and author, the following represent traits of the world's most successful entrepreneurs:
- Have a unique perspective on risk.
- Communicate vision and instill passion.
- Demonstrate resilience and rapid recovery.
- Do what they do best.
- Preserve what they build.
- Knowing when to leave the nest

Have a unique perspective on risk.
Successful entrepreneurs don't take "no" for an answer and don't fear failure. They try new things, implement new ideas and incorporate new strategies in an effort to grow and improve their business. Personal trainers do things that most "conventional" business people wouldn't dare to try. They are not afraid to do something that makes them look silly if they know it will be successful (i.e. new choreography, new (and unconventional) exercises, fun and unique weight loss programs, etc.). They will try anything if they think it will help their clients succeed, help them grow their business, and help them generate more revenue.

Communicate vision and instill passion.
Successful entrepreneurs are able to move an idea and make it reality. Personal trainers do the "impossible" every day with their clients. They take something that is perceived as undesirable (i.e. exercising) and making it fun and enjoyable. They motivate people to improve their lives and their long term quality of life. They change lives every day by

motivating the people they work with by building their self-esteem and the belief they have in themselves.

Demonstrate resilience and rapid recovery.
Personal trainers are put to the test every time they take a client through a session or teach a group training class. Each work day comes with its challenges and opportunities for failure (i.e. starting a client late, getting hurt, stumbling through new choreography, being sick and staying positive, etc.), but personal trainers learn to get back up, learn from their mistakes and move on ... becoming even better than they were before!

Do what they do best.
Personal trainers specialize in an area of expertise. A personal trainer functions very much like a physician with an area of expertise (i.e. general fitness, weight loss, functional training, rehabilitation, sports performance, women's health, active aging, etc.). Their area of knowledge and specialization is what makes them unique and sought out above all others. They are challenged with new clients and unique situations that require confidence and solutions for each individual.

Preserve what they build.
For many entrepreneurs, starting a business is like nurturing a child from birth. There is a personal investment in everything they do on a day to day basis. Personal trainers map out a journey for many people, watching them progress and grow with each interaction. They build connections with clients that are very personal and inherently rewarding.

Knowing When to Leave the Nest
Personal trainers have the character traits to become successful in business. Unfortunately, the majority of them have never ventured down that path. Most of them get started with a fitness club, loving what they do but hardly making enough money to pay the bills. Some consider selling additional products and services to their clients, but many fitness clubs don't allow for sales to occur that don't directly benefit the club. It's a "win-win" situation for the fitness club and a "lose-lose" situation for the personal trainer.

For this reason, many personal trainers don't go the distance. They get frustrated with the "system" and pursue other, more stable and boring, careers.

For the personal trainer who wants to be financially successful (and is brave enough to take the "leap") the logical next step is to start their own personal training business. Unfortunately, many fail to make a decent living because they don't have the business experience or knowledge to do it in a way that can be lucrative and successful.

This doesn't need to be the fate of all personal trainers. The next section will delve deep into the business side of personal training and be the ultimate "how to" guide on developing a successful personal training business with unlimited potential!

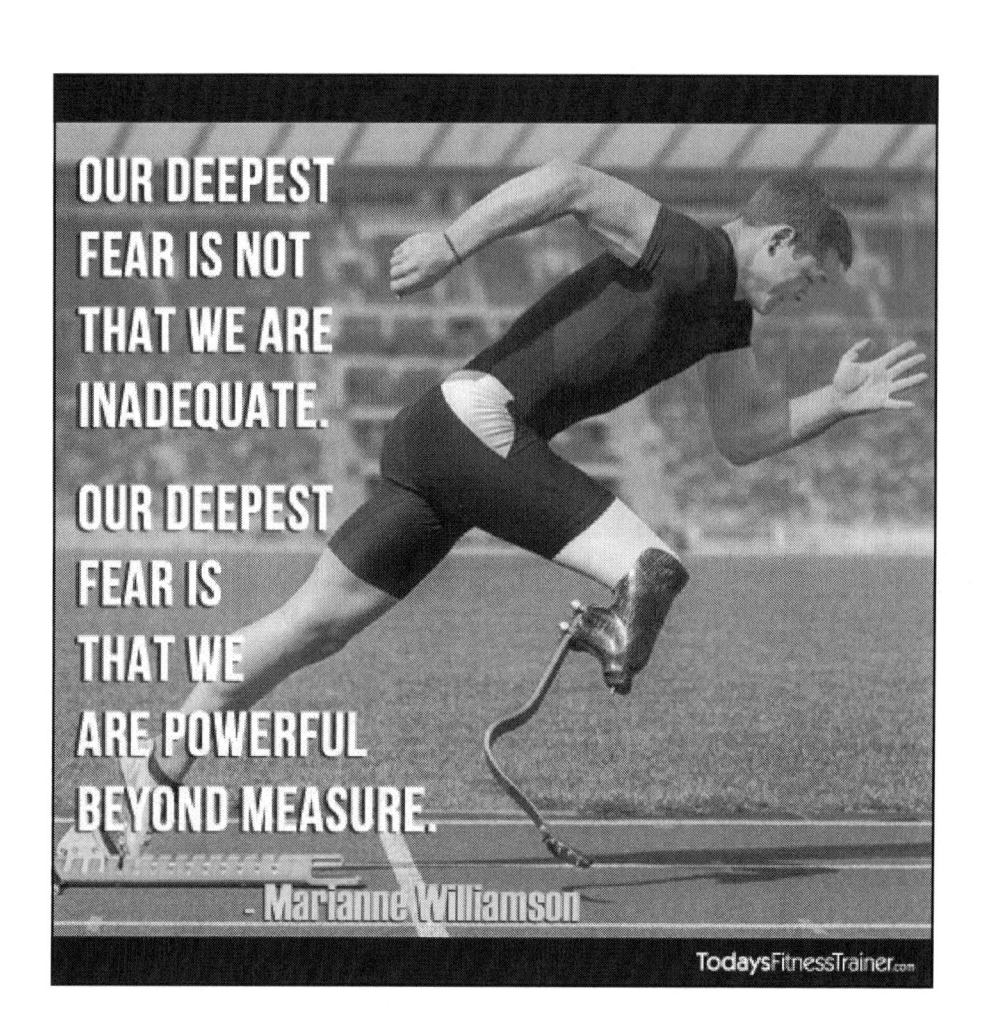

> OUR DEEPEST FEAR IS NOT THAT WE ARE INADEQUATE. OUR DEEPEST FEAR IS THAT WE ARE POWERFUL BEYOND MEASURE.
>
> — Marianne Williamson

PART TWO: BUILDING YOUR PERSONAL TRAINING BUSINESS

If you're reading this part of the book you fall into one of three categories:
1. You've made the decision to become a personal trainer and need to get certified.
2. You're already a personal trainer for a fitness club and want to know how to build your own business.
3. You already operate a personal training business and want to find ways to be more effective, efficient, and more profitable.

The previous chapters provided valuable information about the fitness industry, how fitness culture has changed, the role of personal training and the opportunities that are now available in today's current market. Knowing why and how the industry began and understanding the scope of the industry today provides insight as to where a personal training business can go in the future.

Now that the background research is done, it's time to shift gears and start learning about business and the harsh realities of becoming an entrepreneur. In a perfect world, all entrepreneurs (including personal trainers) would be successful. Unfortunately, only about half of all new businesses survive five years or more and only one-third survive ten years or more (U.S. Small Business Administration, 2012).

There are lots of reasons why businesses fail. It can happen to anyone. However, people who don't have an entrepreneurial mindset are more likely to fail at business than others.

The previous chapter discusses the traits of a successful entrepreneur. Below is a list of characteristics and beliefs of people who are very unlikely to be successful entrepreneurs and are destined for business failure.

They think of work in terms of an hourly wage.
Successful entrepreneurs know that you can't count the worth of your time in terms of dollars and cents. Building a successful business takes a significant amount of time and hard work. In the beginning, the amount of work far outweighs the compensation you make in return. After some time, the balance begins to shift and you make more money with less effort. How long it takes to get to that point depends on many factors (i.e. type of business, business experience, funding, etc.).

They lack patience.
Building a successful business takes time. Similar to changing the body with exercise. You can't expect success overnight. Some people are fortunate and success comes quicker than for others, but it is extremely rare for financial success to come right away. Experts say that it can take up to five years for a new business to be considered financially successful.

They have unreaslistic expectations.
These entrepreneurs expect success and wealth with a minimal investment of time and energy. They believe in "get rich quick" schemes and the role models they focus on are people who claim to have made milions with little to no effort.

They don't understand the importance of action.
Any business does not run by itself, especially a personal training business. If the personal trainer doesn't take action to run, grow or evaluate the business it is destined to fail. The majority of what makes a business successful is dependent on action.

They don't believe in themselves.
Many of the entrepreneurs who fail early in business (and those who never even start) just don't believe they are capable of business success. They lack confidence in themselves and quickly believe the people around them who continually diminish their efforts.

They are afraid.
They are simply afraid of failure. They lose focus on the task at hand and dwell on the negative. For example, they are afraid they won't make enough money to pay their mortgage or feed their children. The think about it constantly and can't get past it.

They think they have one source of income.
This is the clear mark of the non-entrepreneur. If someone with an employee mindset needs more money for anything (to pay bills, to buy a new car), the solution is to get another job or to work more hours. They equate more money to more job. An entrepreneur understands that there are many sources of income. They don't limit themselves to simply doing more of the same. They constantly look for new and different opportunities.

The goal of this guide for successful personal trainers is to help you avoid the pitfalls of starting a new business and "closing your doors" within the first few years. The next chapter begins with looking at developing a strong foundation and structure for your business ... your mission, vision, values, goals and objectives.

Chapter 8:
Planning for Success

At this point you've made the decision to become a personal trainer and to build a successful personal training business. Before you start buying personal training books or dumbbells it's important to structure out your personal training business. It's important to determine the mission, vision, values, goals and objectives of your newly formed business.

Many new business owners don't take the time to clearly outline the vision and future of their business, which clearly limits its ability to succeed. If you can't clearly describe where you're headed there is no way you can expect to get there.

As a first step, think carefully about your new personal training business and try to answer the following questions:
- Is there a clearly identified vision of where your personal training business is headed?
- How will the business look or operate in one, two, five or ten years?
- Do you have a clearly defined mission?
- Why does your business exist?
- What do you hope to achieve?
- Are you personally committed to it?
- Are there specific goals and objectives?

These are not easy questions (and you weren't expected to know the answers right away). If you are determined to build a successful personal training business it is important that you are able to answer them with utmost certainty. To make this process easier, let's break it down into each single component.

Core Values
Core values are the principles and standards at the very center of our character, and from which we do not budge or stray. Core values:
- Are extremely stable and change only very slowly over long periods of time.
- Form the basis for our beliefs about life, ourselves and those around us.
- Form the basis for our beliefs in the human potential of ourselves and others.

Values and beliefs form our attitudes and guide our actions. The behaviors and actions we engage in are what people around us see. This outward display of behaviors and actions can change dramatically throughout life, influenced by our environment and guided by our more stable core values and beliefs.

For some people identifying and communicating personal core values can be a difficult task. Core values are so close to the center of who we are that they tend to be very protected and not shared with others until a personal relationship has been established. The fact that these values are so central to what's important to us individually, makes it all the more important to think about them first as a basis for establishing sound and meaningful mission, vision and goals in both our life and business.

Once you've identified your values (for yourself and your business), it's important to rank them from the most to the least important. This is useful because when questions come up where one value must be traded off against another, the decision will be easier to make. For example, say the core values of a business are safety, respect for others, and efficiency. If a client isn't comfortable being helped or guided through an exercise (i.e. doesn't like to be touched or spotted during exercises) and they are about to drop a weight that is too heavy, the choice is to support the client and assist with the weight. Safety trumps respect for the client's wishes. It won't necessarily make these decisions easy (or totally objective) but it will bring some guidance and consistency to the decision making process.

Defining your core values first will help you get your priorities in order.

Mission
The mission is a broad statement about yourself or the business, including its purpose and operation, that distinguishes you or the business from others. A personal mission statement deals with questions like:
- "Why are we here?"
- "Why do we exist?"
- "Why do we get up each day and do what we do?"
- "What is it that we get paid for?"

A business mission statement deals with questions like:
- "Why does the business exist?"
- "What function does the business perform?"
- "For whom?"
- "How?"

A business mission statement reflects the core values and beliefs of the individual who leads the business. If there are large differences between a business mission and a personal mission, or between business values and personal core values, there will be friction for that individual within the business. One way to help assure happiness and fulfillment at work is to be certain your values and mission are in alignment with those of the business. People have been known to become physically ill from the stress of working in a business where their core values were at odds with the values and ethics practiced in the business.

In addition to giving structure and direction to the personal training business, well-written mission statements are excellent tools to inform others about what's important to you and how the business operates.

Examples of mission statements for personal trainers include:

- *"My priorities are respect for people, excellence and business. Our goal is to be a place where our clients (our most valuable asset) have the opportunity to improve physically, mentally, and spiritually. By putting people first and aspects of the business second, we never veer from the priority of our overall business."*
- *"To provide exceptional personal training experiences for clients as economically as possible. In this way, more people can participate in our programs and the business can generate adequate revenue."*

These two mission statements communicate very different notions about what's important to these two personal training businesses and also give some indication that day-to-day business may be conducted differently as a result.

Any mission statement that concisely represents truth and reality about the individual or the business is a good mission statement. Likewise, any statement that doesn't honestly and accurately represent the values and beliefs of the individual or the personal training business is a poor mission statement, regardless of what is says or how good it sounds. If excellence is a stated value or the pursuit of excellence a stated mission, yet average, industry standard, or legal requirement is "good enough", then what is the real commitment to excellence? Do they really "live" their stated mission?

Mission statements serve to inform other people (i.e. clients, friends, neighbors, and peers) about what's important to you and your business. They also serve as anchors and guideposts for decisons made for the business.

Vision
While a mission is a statement of what is, a vision is a statement of what or how you would like things to be. It's a picture of the future you're working to create and what you want your business to become.

Without a vision of where you're going how can you develop a plan to get there? How will you know when you've arrived? Without a vision of where you would like to be, you may invest time and effort down a specific path only to discover that you've arrived somewhere you really don't want to be.

Nothing was ever created without a vision. It guides us, gives us direction and purpose, and can serve as a powerful motivator for those around us and ourselves. An effective vision must:
- Be aligned with the core values of both the person and the personal training business.
- Be effectively communicated to and accepted by everyone involved in the personal training business (i.e. clients, investors, partners, etc.).

The more precise and detailed you can be in writing a description of your vision of the future, the easier it will be to communicate it to others and gain their commitment to it, and the more likely you will be to achieve it.

Being able to articulate a clear vision of the future is essential if you expect to actually get there. It's even more important if you bring aboard people (i.e. partners, employees or consultants) to ensure they have core values that fit well with the business, and who understand and accept the business mission and vision as matching closely with their own.

Examples of vision statements for personal trainers include:
- "To become the first and most sought after personal training studio in Oregon."
- "To develop world class programs and services that change the face of sports performance training in soccer and lacrosse."
- "To raise funds and give back to the community in the areas of sport and youth development."
- "To become one of the most sought after employers and business partners in the city of Denver."

Goals and Objectives
Mission and vision, although frequently short statements, are broad, encompassing and far-reaching. They can often seem overwhelming and perhaps even impossible to achieve. The metaphor, "A journey

of a thousand miles begins with the first step.", fits well in regard to achieving a mission and vision. Goals and objectives create the road map and manageable stepping stones to achieve the mission, make the vision a reality, and navigate the course you set for your personal training business, and for yourself.

The terms "goal" and "objective" are often confused with each other. They both describe things that a person may want to achieve or attain but, in relative terms, may mean different things. Both are desired outcomes of work done by a person but what sets them apart is the time frame, attributes they're set for, and the overall result. A goal is "the purpose toward which an endeavor is directed" and an objective is "something that one's efforts or actions are intended to attain or accomplish (i.e. a purpose or target)". Regardless of what we call them, it's important to break things into smaller pieces and then "break it down to microscopic" in terms of identifying the steps that will move us in the direction you want (and need) to go. While it's possible to get bogged down in the small details, the reality is, few people error on the side of too much detail when it comes to writing goals and objectives. More often than not people are confused and frustrated by a lack of detail.

To be effective, goals and objectives must be written down. If they aren't in writing they're merely ideas with no real power or conviction behind them. Written goals and objectives provide motivation to achieve them and then act as a reminder to you (and others). Clearly and specifically written, they also eliminate confusion and misunderstanding.

A useful way of effectively outlining focused goals and objectives is by using the S.M.A.R.T. principle (specific, measurable, achievable, relevant, and time-bound):
- Specific: Make sure your goal or objective specifies what needs to be done (i.e. actions and activities) and a timeline for completion (i.e. number of days or a specific date).
- Measurable: Your goal or objective should include numbers or descriptions that measure quantity (i.e. number of sessions booked or amount of revenue

BE S.M.A.R.T.!
SET EFFECTIVE GOALS TO HELP YOU STAY ON TRACK ALL YEAR LONG!

S — Your goal must be clear and specific.

M — Your goal must be measurable.

A — Your goal must be attainable.

R — Your goal must be realistic.

T — Your goal must have a timeline (or deadline) attached to it.

TodaysFitnessTrainer.com

- Attainable: generated).
 Your goal or objective should be something that is under your direct control. Do you have access to resources to help you achieve your goal? Can your goal be reached in the timeframe you've outlined? Is it achievable and truly attainable?
- Realistic: Your goal or objective should be reasonable and something that is under your direct control. Do you have access to resources to help you achieve your goal? Can your goal be reached in the timeframe you've outlined?
- Time-Bound: Your goal or objective should identify a definite target date or timeline for completion.

Among all the attributes of a well-written goal or objective, the most important are measurable results and a timeframe for completion. Being able to quantify results and evaluate the timeliness of accomplishing goals gives you the opportunity to assess the performance and progress of the overall business.

Having well developed goals and objectives also helps:
- Maintain focus and perspective.
- Establish priorities.
- Lead to greater job satisfaction.
- Improve employee performance.

Over time as goals are achieved, or conditions and situations change, it's important to reevaluate and establish new goals and objectives. This ensures your business will not get stale and continue to grow and progress forward.

Your Homework Assisgnment
1. Write out your core values. ☐
2. Write out your mission statement. ☐
3. Write out your vision statement. ☐
4. Write out your goals for the business ☐
5. Write out the objectives that will help you accomplish each of the goals outlined. ☐

Table 9-2

American College of Sports Medicine (ACSM)

NAME	American College of Sports Medicine
WEBSITE	www.acsm.org
ESTABLISHED	1954
INDUSTRY RECOGNITION	High
CERTIFICATION	Certified Personal Trainer (CPT)
COURSE LOCATION(S)	United States (major cities)
COURSE DURATION	1 day workshop, 3 day course, or 6 session webinar
COURSE COST	$129 USD, $375 USD, or $240 USD
MATERIALS COST	$135 USD
PREREQUISITE(S)	High School Diploma, Adult CPR Certificate
EXAM COST	$219 USD (member) $279 USD (non-member)
RETEST COST	$150 USD
EXAM DURATION	2.5 hours
EXAM QUESTIONS	120 scored + 30 unscored
EXAM LOCATION(S)	Worldwide
TIME (course + exam)	4 to 9 months

* Updated June 30, 2013. Information subject to change without notice. *

Table 9-3

American Council on Exercise (ACE)

NAME	American Council on Exercise
WEBSITE	www.acefitness.org
ESTABLISHED	1985
INDUSTRY RECOGNITION	High
CERTIFICATION	Personal Trainer
COURSE LOCATION(S)	United States (major cities)
COURSE DURATION	2 days
COURSE COST	$399 USD
MATERIALS COST	Included
PREREQUISITE(S)	18 years old, Adult CPR/AED Certificate
EXAM COST	$219 USD (pencil/paper) $249 USD (computer)
RETEST COST	$135 USD (pencil/paper) $184 USD (computer)
EXAM DURATION	3 hours
EXAM QUESTIONS	150
EXAM LOCATION(S)	Worldwide
TIME (course + exam)	3 to 6 months

* *Updated June 30, 2013. Information subject to change without notice.* *

Table 9-4

Canadian Fitness Professionals (CanFitPro)

NAME	Canadian Fitness Professionals
WEBSITE	www.canfitpro.com
ESTABLISHED	1993
INDUSTRY RECOGNITION	Moderate - High
CERTIFICATION	Personal Training Specialist (CPT)
COURSE LOCATION(S)	Canada (major cities)
COURSE DURATION	27 hours
COURSE COST	$449 CDN (member) $573 CDN (non-member)
MATERIALS COST	Included
PREREQUISITE(S)	16 years old, Adult CPR Certificate
EXAM COST	Included
RETEST COST	$75 CDN
EXAM DURATION	3 hours
EXAM QUESTIONS	100
EXAM LOCATION(S)	Canada (major cities
TIME (course + exam)	4 to 6 weeks

* *Updated June 30, 2013. Information subject to change without notice.* *

Table 9-5

International Fitness Professional Association (IFPA)

NAME	International Fitness Professional Association
WEBSITE	www.ifpa-fitness.com
ESTABLISHED	1994
INDUSTRY RECOGNITION	Moderate - High
CERTIFICATION	Certified Personal Trainer (CPT)
COURSE LOCATION(S)	United States (major cities)
COURSE DURATION	2 days
COURSE COST	$399 to $459 USD
MATERIALS COST	Included
PREREQUISITE(S)	High School Diploma, 18 years old, Adult CPR Certificate
EXAM COST	Included
RETEST COST	$79 USD
EXAM DURATION	2.5 hours
EXAM QUESTIONS	100
EXAM LOCATION(S)	Worldwide
TIME (course + exam)	3 to 6 months

* Updated June 30, 2013. Information subject to change without notice. *

Table 9-6

International Sports Sciences Association (ISSA)

NAME	International Sports Sciences Association
WEBSITE	www.issaonline.edu
ESTABLISHED	1988
INDUSTRY RECOGNITION	Moderate - High
CERTIFICATION	Certified Personal Trainer (CPT) - Self Paced
COURSE LOCATION(S)	Online
COURSE DURATION	10 weeks (or undergraduate course option)
COURSE COST	$624 to $925 USD
MATERIALS COST	Included
PREREQUISITE(S)	High School Diploma, 18 years old, Adult CPR/AED Certificate
EXAM COST	Not Applicable
RETEST COST	$50 USD (first retest if FREE)
EXAM DURATION	Not available
EXAM QUESTIONS	Not available
EXAM LOCATION(S)	Online & United States (locations)
TIME (course + exam)	Up to 8 months (to complete the course)

* Updated June 30, 2013. Information subject to change without notice. *

Table 9-7

National Academy of Sports Medicine (NASM)

NAME	National Academy of Sports Medicine
WEBSITE	www.nasm.org
ESTABLISHED	1987
INDUSTRY RECOGNITION	High
CERTIFICATION	Certified Personal Trainer (CPT)
COURSE LOCATION(S)	United States (select cities)
COURSE DURATION	2 days
COURSE COST	$629 to $799 USD
MATERIALS COST	Included
PREREQUISITE(S)	18 years old, Adult CPR/AED Certificate
EXAM COST	Included
RETEST COST	$199 USD
EXAM DURATION	2 hours
EXAM QUESTIONS	120
EXAM LOCATION(S)	United States (major cities)
TIME (course + exam)	4 to 6 months

* Updated June 30, 2013. Information subject to change without notice. *

Table 9-8
National Council on Strength and Fitness (NCSF)

NAME	National Council on Strength and Fitness
WEBSITE	www.ncsf.org
ESTABLISHED	1999
INDUSTRY RECOGNITION	High
CERTIFICATION	Certified Personal Trainer (CPT)
COURSE LOCATION(S)	United States (major cities
COURSE DURATION	2 days (or extended school option)
COURSE COST	$309 USD
MATERIALS COST	Included
PREREQUISITE(S)	None
EXAM COST	$199 USD
RETEST COST	$135 USD
EXAM DURATION	3 hours
EXAM QUESTIONS	150
EXAM LOCATION(S)	United States and Canada (400 locations)
TIME (course + exam)	4 to 6 months

* *Updated June 30, 2013. Information subject to change without notice.* *

Table 9-9

National Exercise and Sports Trainers Association (NESTA)

NAME	National Exercise & Sports Trainers Association
WEBSITE	www.nestacertified.com
ESTABLISHED	1992
INDUSTRY RECOGNITION	Moderate
CERTIFICATION	Personal Fitness Trainer (PFT)
COURSE LOCATION(S)	United States (major cities
COURSE DURATION	2 days
COURSE COST	$648 USD (w/POLAR watch) $449 USD (no watch)
MATERIALS COST	Included
PREREQUISITE(S)	18 years old,, High School Diploma (or equivalent)
EXAM COST	$199 USD
RETEST COST	$95 USD
EXAM DURATION	2 hours
EXAM QUESTIONS	100
EXAM LOCATION(S)	United States (major cities)
TIME (course + exam)	4 to 6 weeks

* Updated June 30, 2013. Information subject to change without notice. *

Table 9-10
National Federation of Personal Trainers (NFPT)

NAME	National Federation of Personal Trainers
WEBSITE	www.nfpt.com
ESTABLISHED	1988
INDUSTRY RECOGNITION	Moderate - High
CERTIFICATION	Certified Personal Trainer (CPT)
COURSE LOCATION(S)	United States (major cities)
COURSE DURATION	2 days
COURSE COST	$579 USD (full package) $329 USD (exam only)
MATERIALS COST	Included
PREREQUISITE(S)	High School Diploma, 18 years old, 2+ years fitness experience
EXAM COST	$44 USD
RETEST COST	$60 USD
EXAM DURATION	2 hours
EXAM QUESTIONS	120
EXAM LOCATION(S)	Worldwide (350 locations)
TIME (course + exam)	2 to 6 months

* *Updated June 30, 2013. Information subject to change without notice.* *

Table 9-11
National Personal Training Institute

NAME	National Personal Training Institute
WEBSITE	www.nptifitness.com
ESTABLISHED	2000
INDUSTRY RECOGNITION	High
CERTIFICATION	Diploma in Personal Training + NASM-CPT
COURSE LOCATION(S)	United States and Canada (30+ locations)
COURSE DURATION	500 hours
COURSE COST	$5900 to $6300 USD
MATERIALS COST	Included
PREREQUISITE(S)	18 years old, U.S. Citizen/Green Card, High School Diploma
EXAM COST	$199 USD
RETEST COST	$135 USD
EXAM DURATION	3 hours
EXAM QUESTIONS	150
EXAM LOCATION(S)	United States and Canada (400 locations)
TIME (course + exam)	4 to 12 months

* *Updated June 30, 2013. Information subject to change without notice.* *

Table 9-12
National Strength and Conditioning Association (NSCA)

NAME	National Strength and Conditioning Association
WEBSITE	www.nsca-lift.org
ESTABLISHED	1993
INDUSTRY RECOGNITION	High
CERTIFICATION	NSCA-Certified Personal Trainer (NSCA-CPT)
COURSE LOCATION(S)	Worldwide (limited cities); online exam (US only)
COURSE DURATION	Not applicable
COURSE COST	Not applicable
MATERIALS COST	Up to $468 USD
PREREQUISITE(S)	18 years old, Adult CPR/AED Certificate, High School Diploma
EXAM COST	$235 to $405 USD (written) $285 to $420 USD (computer-based)
RETEST COST	$185 to $355 USD (written) $235 to $370 USD (computer-based)
EXAM DURATION	3 hours
EXAM QUESTIONS	140
EXAM LOCATION(S)	Worldwide (written), United States (computer)
TIME (course + exam)	4 to 9 months

* *Updated June 30, 2013. Information subject to change without notice.* *

Chapter 10:
Building Experience

Congratulations! You're now a certified personal trainer! The countless hours you've invested in learning the valuable information that will prepare you for your new career finally paid off! You even have the certificate to prove it. So, now what?!?!?

The piece of paper you now have in your hand, endorsed by an accredited personal training organization, is similar to a driver's permit for someone learning to drive a car. Just like the personal training certification course, you need to pass the written test to earn the right to legally drive a vehicle under the supervision of a licensed driver. Law enforcement officers penalize individuals who break the law in an effort to maintain a safe environment for other drivers on the road.

Like the person who gets a driver's permit, a newly certified personal trainer is knowledgeable in the area of fitness and exercise, but has no real experience in delivering services. These personal trainers are both dangerous to their clients and to their new business.

Because a personal trainer is responsible for the safety of their clients you would think there would be strict measures to monitor the quality of personal trainers in the market. Unfortunately, the same licensing process doesn't exist for personal trainers.

Although this one step process makes it much easier to get started, new personal trainers are clearly set up to fail. This is because knowledge alone is not enough to be effective. Interpersonal skills and the ability to build trust and loyalty are more important, in the long run, when it comes to selling services and building repeat business through a growing base of loyal clients.

In order to sell personal training services effectively, the following are required:
- Knowledge, skills and abilities
- Interpersonal skills
- Credibility
- Practice ... practice ... practice ...

Knowledge, Skills, and Abilities
Personal trainers require the knowledge, skills, and abilities to be successful. Certification courses provide the information required to become a good personal trainer. The skills and abilities, on the other hand, are the responsibility of the personal trainer to acquire and master.

The skills and abilities personal trainers need to be successful include:
- Effective application of personal training knowledge to the needs of the client
- Effective communication skills (the ability to listen carefully and speak clearly)
- The ability to motivate a client to perform exercise
- The ability to demonstrate the exercises and activities effectively (and with proper form)
- The ability to develop customized programs for their clients
- Effective time management skills
- Exceptional selling skills (see Chapter 14)

These skills and abilities may take weeks, months or years to master. It's up to each personal trainer to cultivate these skills in preparation for the opening of their own business (one that offers services people will be willing to buy).

Interpersonal Skills

You have to keep in mind, "personal training is personal". People who choose to spend their hard earned dollars on personal training do so because of the personal attention and care, motivation, and connection they have with someone they trust as they sweat through the workouts. These are skills that can't be taught in text books or by taking an online course.

Personal training clients are looking for more than just a well thought out exercise program. They are looking for more than a fitness book, workout DVD, or streaming online videos (i.e. YouTube.com or DailyBurn.com). They are ultimately looking for someone to hold them accountable to the work required to achieve their fitness goals.

Credibility
Generally, people don't buy from people they don't trust. This is the reason why all personal trainers, new or veterans in the field, need to establish credibility in order to be successful. This is done by consistently demonstrating credibility and expertise as a personal trainer over time. This can be done by the following:
- Demonstrating your capabilities as a personal trainer
- Establishing a track record of your results (and those of your clients)
- Building rapport and strengthening relationships

The first step to building credibility is to establish clients to begin generating the experience needed to build on.

Practice. Practice. Practice.
The best learning comes from trial and error and the experiences of others in the same field. Like a precious diamond, highly valued and in exceeding demand, time and pressure is required.

There is no set amount of time for this process to take place, as each person learns differently and at their own pace. In general terms, more time is always better than less. In the end, the more experience you have, and the more clients you have "under your belt", the more valuable you become. The last thing you want is to make a careless mistake that puts your business in jeopardy early in your new career.

There are several ways to gain experience and strategically build your value as a personal trainer:
- Volunteer your services
- Become an intern
- Become an employee (fitness club/training studio)
- Become an independent contractor (fitness club/training studio)

Volunteer
At the beginning, new personal trainers have little to no credibility with

To SUCCEED you must first improve.

To IMPROVE you must first practice.

To PRACTICE you must first learn.

To LEARN you must first fail.

paying customers, especially if they have no employer to vouch for their abilities. Volunteering your services to a handful of individuals (for a limited time) gives you the opportunity to gain valuable experience and have others speak to your abilities as a personal trainer.

Volunteers that you hand pick should be within your immediate circle of influence and should be individuals that you personally trust and who will be open and honest with you for feedback and constructive criticism. These individuals may include:
- Family members
- Close friends
- Co-workers
- Other fitness professionals (i.e. personal trainers, fitness instructors)

Be sure to have them provide you with a testimonial and the authorization (in writing) to use their information on printed materials or your website as a way to market your services as a personal trainer.

Internship
Internship programs provide supervised practical experience for people wanting to gain hands-on knowledge as a personal trainer. Although they can be time consuming and without compensation, internship programs (unpaid or paid) can provide some of the best experience for a new personal trainer. You work closely with an experienced personal trainer, in a real working environment, with real training clients seeking help.

An unpaid internship program is designed to allow recent graduates from college, university or personal training certification courses to observe the practical skills they will need to work successfully with clients in the future. Typically, interns are allowed to observe a personal trainer (or mentor) facilitating training sessions in exchange for cleaning, maintenance and/or administrative work.

A paid internship program, on the other hand, consists of more specific responsibilities for both the personal trainers (or mentors) and the students. In this type of program, students pay a program fee in exchange for in depth, hands-on experience and education in the area of personal training.

Employee
Many personal trainers start their career as an employee of a fitness club or personal training studio. Although the employer may not provide the salary or wages you would expect running your own business, there are many benefits that may come with the job, including:
- Salary (and commissions)
- Marketing
- Systems
- Administration
- The ability to learn from other personal trainers
- The ability to network
- Potential liability insurance coverage
- Continuing education opportunities (paid for by the employer)

Independent Contractor
An independent contractor is a business owner who makes their own schedule but utilizes the facility of a gym and/or studio owner to offset the cost of property, land and/or equipment. They pay the facility owner for the time in the facility (like rent to use their building and equipment) to train their personal training clients. The personal trainer can charge clients whatever they want, paying the facility a flat fee per month or a per-client fee. An independent contractor can make more money than an employee, but is also responsible for marketing, taxes and other business costs.

Regardless of which route you choose, each experience will make you a better and more valuable personal trainer as you work towards your own business and your own facility. No rent. No limitations. Just you ... helping other people and creating a career worth pursuing for the long term.

But, at the same time, don't be in a rush to start your own business. Whether you are getting paid or not, your value increases with each learning experience. Use your time wisely, see as many different clients as you can and continue to fine tune your business strategy and grand opening plan.

Your Homework Assignment
1. Write down the names of all your close friends, family members and colleagues. ☐
2. From the list, choose ten (10) people you would like to offer complimentary personal training in exchange for feedback and testimonials. ☐
3. Write down the names of local personal trainer(s) and/or facilities you would like to work with. ☐
4. Draft your current resume to reflect your knowledge, skills and abilities in the field of personal training. ☐
5. Choose the best option to build personal training experience. Put into action! ☐

Chapter 11:
Creating Your Personal Brand

According to the Bureau of Labor Statistics, there were over 250,000 fitness trainers and aerobics instructors employed in the United States in 2010. That number is expected to increase 24% by 2020 to over 310,000 fitness professionals. In a highly competitive market with lots of competition, how does one differentiate themselves from the pack and be successful? Personal branding.

Your personal brand is the powerful, clear, positive idea that comes to mind whenever people think of you. It's what you represent (your values, abilities and actions) that others associate with you. Your personal brand influences how others perceive you in your work environment, including your clients, colleagues and competitors. It does this by telling your clients/potential clients three (3) things:
- Who you are as a personal trainer.
- What you do as a personal trainer.
- What makes you different from other personal trainers (or how you create value for your clients).

Many contacts in your circle of influence may already hold a high opinion of you based on these qualities, even though you weren't even trying. So ... imagine what would happen if you consciously crafted your personal brand to demonstrate your value to the people you want to work with (and those who can influence others to work with you)!

A Personal Brand is About Influence

Essentially, a personal brand is about influence. Personal brands influence how potential clients perceive you. Ideally, your personal brand will match the characteristics that your potential clients find valuable. This builds a sense of comfort and confidence when looking for a personal trainer. To be effective, your personal brand must elicit the following three messages in the minds of your potential client:

1. You are different.
   To be seen as new and original is the most important aspect of personal branding.
2. You are superior.
   Your personal brand must encourage the belief that you are the among the best at what you do in some way (training ability, interaction with clients, get proven results, knowledge and experience, etc.).
3. You are authentic.
   Great personal brands are genuine and real. Your personal brand must be built on the truth of who you are, what your strength is, and what you love about your work as a personal trainer.

Your personal brand tells potential clients what they can expect when they train with you, which is what makes it so powerful. It's an implied commitment between a personal trainer and a client (a promise that makes the client believe that when they pay for personal training, they are getting what they expect in return). People buy because a consumer brand (i.e. Apple, Starbucks, Nordstrom) makes them feel a certain way and their choices are rarely rational. Brands create expectations, and if those expectations are met, people will buy again (aka. brand loyalty). If the brand doesn't live up to a person's expectations, they will go somewhere else.

A personal brand works the same way. How you perform in your job throughout the day broadcasts information about your character, abilities and performance. It creates expectations in the minds of others of what they'll get when they work with you. If your personal brand is sending the right message, potential clients won't have a single reason to look elsewhere when they are looking for a personal trainer.

Creating a Successful Personal Brand
Start by identifying the qualities and characteristics that make you distinctive from your competitors. Ask yourself the following questions:
- What have you done recently (i.e. the last week) to make yourself stand out as a personal trainer?
- What would your clients or colleagues say is your greatest strength as a personal trainer?
- What is your most noteworthy/distinguishing personal trait that makes you a great personal trainer?

Next take these qualities and characteristics and identify the benefits each one has to your personal training clients. An example would look like this:

"My experience as a mother of two young children, staying fit and healthy through two pregnancies, makes me a more effective personal trainer for women looking to remain active during their pregnancy in addition to helping them get back into shape post-preganancy."

Once you've identified the benefits you distinctively bring to your clients, you need to create your personal brand message. This is essentially the "30 second sales pitch" that is consistent in all of your marketing efforts as you sell your services as the "right" personal trainer for your target market. This message needs to be honest, genuine and sincere. An example would look like this:

"My name is Jack and I am a certified personal trainer of two years. I've had the pleasure of working with, and learning from, the greatest fitness mentors in the industry. I continue loving to learn as I work towards improving with each new client. Getting results is important to my clients but my number one concern is safety and creating positive fitness experiences. My clients would say my best traits are my attention to detail and how I make the workouts challenging and fun!"

Regardless of how you communicate your personal brand message as a personal trainer (i.e. in conversation, in writing, on the radio, or in a video) it's important that the message matches the expectations of the audience for the optimal effect. For example, a personal trainer with a personal brand associated with youth and family fitness could organize an after school group walking program in their neighborhood or work with their local church group to provide fitness programs and services. Your personal brand is what you say, how you act and how others perceive you as a personal trainer.

Developing a great personal brand can ultimately:
- Get you more of the right type of clients.
- Increase your earning potential. Your personal brand will position you as one of the leaders as a personal trainer (you'll be able to demand a higher pay).
- Create a consistent flow of business.
- Keep you "top of mind" when people are looking for a personal trainer.
- Increase your credibility as a personal trainer.
- Create added perceived value as a personal trainer.
- Get you recognized.

As a personal trainer there are three things you need to do to become successful:
1. You have to provide real value to your client.
2. You have to be a personal training "visionary" (a leader, a teacher, and an "imagineer" – being able to imagine and create something bold and new).
3. You have to be a businessperson (focused on the processes to generate revenue).

Create your brand. Create your plan. Plant the seeds and watch your business grow!

Your Homework Assignment
1. Ask yourself, "Who am I?". Write down your answer ☐ (refer to your core values, mission, and vision).
2. Ask yourself, "What do I do in business?". Write down ☐ your answer.
3. Ask yourself, "What makes me different from my ☐

competitors?". Write down your answer.
4. Ask yourself, "What have I done recently to distinguish myself from my competitors?". Write down your answer. ☐
5. Ask yourself, "What are my greatest strengths as a personal trainer (in the eyes of my clients)?". Write down your answer. ☐
6. Ask yourself, "What is my most noteworthy/distinguishable personal trait that makes me a great personal trainer?". Write down your answer. ☐
7. Write out your "30 Second Sales Pitch" (using the information gathered in the previous steps). ☐

Chapter 12:
Building Your Business

A successful personal training business is less about a person's ability to provide personal training services than it is about running a well structured and streamlined business. Any service-based business (i.e. Starbucks, 24 Hour Fitness or Massage Envy) drives ongoing success based on the following:
- Brand identity and value proposition
- High quality products and services
- Quality relationships with customers

Without these elements, a business will struggle to differentiate itself against competitors and drive a high value for the services they sell. Personal trainers need to understand how to create a need for their services at a high dollar value to motivate people to buy (and continue buying). These items listed above make up the framework of an effective business plan (an important first step in the development of any successful business). When developing your business plan and strategy it is useful to ask the following questions:
- What is the distinctive brand value of my personal training business?
- What are the products and services that I will offer?
- How will I differentiate my business from the competition (i.e. specialization, value-added services, proprietary programs, etc.)?

- How will I drive sales and referrals for the business?
- How will I develop long-lasting relationships with my customers?
- What are the measures of success that I will evaluate my performance against?

By completing the homework assignments in the previous chapters, you are already prepared to begin tackling the next step, the business plan.

Rules and Guidelines of the Business
Rules are important because it lets society know what is expected of them. If you break the rules there are consequences and you are aware of that as well. Rules keep us in order.

Rules make up the foundation of society. They set expectations and guidelines for order and control in our everyday lives. Without rules there would be chaos and we would suffer from a wide variety of negative consequences. If we live by rules in our everyday lives (i.e. on the road, at work, at school, in sports) it would only make sense to have rules and guidelines in business as well.

A business plan outlines the rules and guidelines of the business. A good business plan follows generally accepted guidelines and is broken down into three primary sections:
1. Business concept: Information about the industry, your business structure, your particular product or service, and how you plan to make your business a success.
2. Marketplace section: Information about potential customers (who and where they are, what makes them buy, etc.), competition and how the business will position itself against them.
3. Financial section: Information about your income and cash flow, balance sheet and other financial reports. This part may require help from your accountant and a good spreadsheet software program.

Breaking these three major sections down even further, a business plan

consists of seven key components:
1. Executive summary
2. Business description
3. Market strategies (including sales)
4. Competitive analysis
5. Design and development plan
6. Operations and management plan
7. Financial factors

In addition to these sections, a business plan should also have a cover, title page and table of contents. This guide was written to provide personal trainers with the information and tools needed to draft a well thought out and thorough business plan.

Although all sections of the business plan are important, two areas of great importance that truly differentiate one business concept from another is in the market strategies (including sales) and the operation and management plan. These sections "make or break" a business.

Market Strategies

A marketing strategy serves to develop a competitive advantage in the marketplace and to implement an effective plan and generate revenues to support day-to-day operations of the business. A strategy that ensures a consistent approach to outselling the competition is critical. But the strategy is useless unless there is a way to consistently implement it successfully for the long term. Examples include:
- Website content and design
- Social media platforms and communication initiatives (i.e. Facebook, Twitter, Pinterest)
- Customer testimonials and recognition
- Contests and promotions
- Community outreach (i.e. fundraising events, sporting events, school presentations)

Sales Strategies

Most people are not born to sell … yet sales is what ensures a business can thrive. In essence, a business must seek every opportunity to win sales, through competitive advantages, in order to survive. A strategic sales strategy is essential to maximize one's time and effort to generate sales.

Selling consists of two main functions: strategy and tactics. A strategic sales strategy is the planning of sales activities (i.e. methods of reaching clients, sales materials and resources). Examples include:
- eNewsletter broadcast to all current and past clients once per month
- Referral incentive for all clients that complete "x" personal training sessions
- Gift baskets, raffles and rewards
- "Give the Gift of Fitness" promotion (December 1 to 31)
- "Buy 10 Get 2 FREE (for a friend)" promotion
- "Bridal Bootcamp" promotion (April 1 to August 31)
- Facebook "Why I Need a Personal Trainer" contest (win 10 sessions with a personal trainer)

Tactics involves the actual day-to-day selling (i.e. prospecting, sales process and follow-up). Examples include:
- Selling sheet (outlines pricing and value proposition)
- Website (online shopping cart)
- Groupon or Living Social campaign
- Group or fundraiser classes to build leads/prospect lists

Operations and Management
Operations and management processes are designed to ensure the business is efficient in its operations by ensuring quality control, minimizing costs and maximizing revenue. This includes the following:
- Effective scheduling of client appointments and classes (i.e. client access to online scheduling and payment)
- Identifying location(s) where services are offered (i.e. private studio, in home, local park, etc.)
- Customer surveys and feedback
- Management of employees, volunteers and partners
- Maintaining insurance and memberships (i.e. certifications, CPR/First Aid)
- Accounting and finance (i.e. to provide information about the business to make sound financial decisions)

- Evaluation and re-structuring of the business (at regularly timed intervals)

In summary, there is a big difference between being a personal trainer employed by a fitness company and starting your own personal training business. Personal trainers that take the time and make the effort to develop a strong business plan have a much greater change of developing a business that will succeed and thrive in a market that is willing to pay for health driven results. Not only does your business come across as more established and credible, you can price your services at a higher value and cultivate clients that are loyal and who become the foundation of your growing business.

Entrepreneurs are not looking to "buy a job". Entrepreneurs are looking to develop something that gives them a life worth living and a legacy to leave behind through their work. Effective planning gives you the opportunity to enjoy your career, maintain a manageable schedule, generate significant revenues … and still have time to enjoy the pleasures that life has to offer!

Your Homework Assignment
1. Write down the products and services you plan on offering (i.e. single sessions, session packages, complete programs, etc.). ☐
2. Write down the value (price) for each product and service. ☐
3. Write down marketing strategies and ideas for future consideration. ☐
4. Write down operations and management processes and procedures for the personal training business. ☐

Chapter 13:
Marketing Your Brand

Marketing is not rocket science (although many people new in business are afraid of it). Marketing shouldn't be feared ... it should be embraced. Marketing is truly the "life blood" of sales (because they don't happen easily with out it).

Marketing, in the simplest terms, is an activity. These activities and strategies result in making products and services available to satisfy the needs of customers while making profits for the business providing the products and services.

The primary goal of marketing is to create enough interest to make the "phone ring, the inbox ding, and the door swing". Marketing will not sell services or personal training session. Marketing makes selling easier. In the end, selling is your job! With that thought in mind, consider that there are really only three things you can offer to entice your potential clients:
1. Time
2. Money
3. Free stuff

Time
People are more likely to buy something if they can try it first, without

risk. Whether it is a free trial session or one at a significant discount (i.e. Groupon, LivingSocial), the trial session offers you a way to create and establish value while removing a barrier of entry. It gives you the opportunity to earn a potential client's business (without high-pressure sales tactics) and show them how you can help change their life.

Money
Low-priced personal trainers thrive on this type of offer and high-valued personal trainers despise it. Price can be used effectively, but it must be done strategically. Too many times a personal trainer thinks a "percent discount" or "pay only $$$" offer is great, but they forget to include the perceived value of the offer to the potential client. Below are two versions of the same offer:
- Bad example: "Purchase a 10 pack of personal training sessions, receive a fitness assessment and bioimpedance analysis for FREE!"
- Good example: "Purchase a 10 pack of personal training sessions, receive a fitness assessment and bioimpedance analysis for FREE! A value of over $200!"

Promotional offers should be done strategically and sparingly. If discounts and promotions are offered on an ongoing basis, there is no real value for the services and clients expect they can negotiate for the lowest price all the time.

Free Stuff
People love free stuff, especially in a slow economy when a lot of people aren't buying. This is a "win-win" situation for both you and your potential client because you maintain full value of your services and you add value to your client. For example, "Purchase a 10 pack of personal training sessions and receive a t-shirt, water bottle and one personal training session to give to a friend or family member". The offer must provide a real value to the potential client. A suite of products and services are more appealing than just one item.

Communicating the Marketing Message
Developing the right marketing message is one thing. Communicating it to your potential clients is something entirely different. With more

than 5,000 marketing messages bombarding us each day, getting your message across can be challenging.

You can't control when and why a potential client decides to buy. But, if they don't know you even exist, or that you have an enticing offer for them to consider, they have no reason to buy from you. In order to stack the deck in your favor, the goal is to put your marketing message into as many hands as possible (in a consistent and frequent manner).

You need to establish ownership of that spot in their mind, as the solution for their personal training needs, so they come directly to you when they are ready to buy.

There are three different avenues to deliver your marketing message and reach your intended audience (to get them to actively contact you):
 1. Online marketing (website, Facebook, Twitter, etc.)
 2. Direct marketing (direct mail, handouts, flyers, vouchers)
 3. Face to face (trade shows, workshops, seminars)

Online Marketing
Reaching potential clients using online marketing is all about commitment and strategy. Online marketing involves the use of digital media to inform the market of your business and to entice people to purchase your products and services. The Internet (including mobile) is just a vehicle to provide greater reach for your advertising and promotional efforts. Online marketing should be a part of your overall marketing plan.

Businesses that want to boost the results of traditional advertising need to include Internet strategies as well. A good Internet site, for example, improves the effectiveness of other advertising because many customers who see your company's advertising will evaluate your company's products and services online. Integrating Internet marketing tactics with other advertising ensures that your company provides a consistent brand experience.

You should consider the following when developing your overall online marketing strategy:

- Business website
- Social media
- Content marketing

Business Website

Every type of business needs to have a website. It's just as important as a phone number or physical address. You wouldn't be in business long if people didn't have a way to contact you. Business websites are increasingly becoming an expected connecting point between you and your potential clients. The Internet is also a place for small businesses to represent themselves and be accessible 24/7 throughout the year. Below are 7 reasons why you should get quality web design for your personal training business.

1. A business website introduces potential clients to you.
   A business website provides new businesses with much needed exposure to new customers. When your business is on the web, anyone in the world can connect and find your business.
2. Creating a website establishes trust.
   When you create a business website, you are telling people that you are serious about your business. You are welcoming them to use your services and you are establishing trust.
3. Having a business website gets you listed on search engines.
   Search engines (i.e. Google, Bing, Yahoo) are used by over 90% of adults. In fact, Google averaged over 5 billion searches per day in 2012! In addition, studies show that most people's first exposure to a new business will initiate from an online search. So if your business isn't showing up in search engine results pages, you are effectively hiding your business from potential customers.
4. Having a website provides a great first impression.
   People associate your business with your website. If you have a great looking website that is well organized and easy to navigate, people will have a good impression about your business.
5. A business website is a great "connection point" for your business.
   With a well designed website, potential clients will be able to easily contact you, review your services and be kept up to date with the latest news and information about your personal training business. Your potential customers can sign up to follow your website and receive information via email.

6. A business website helps you leverage social networking sites.
   A business website can take advantage of popular social networking sites like Facebook, Google+ and Twitter. When your website integrates with social networking sites you're able to reach a larger audience to promote your business.
7. A business website works for you 24/7.
   The Internet never sleeps so your website is open for business 24/7. It introduces your company to potential clients, tells them your story and sells them your services ... on their timeline. You don't have to go out and sell. The website can do that for you.

Social Media

Social media marketing refers to the process of gaining website traffic or attention through social media sites. Popular social media sites include:
- Facebook
- Twitter
- LinkedIn
- Google+
- Pinterest

Social media marketing programs focus their efforts on creating content that attracts attention and encourages readers to share it with their own social networks. A targeted message spreads from user to user and resonates because it comes from a trusted source, as opposed to the brand or company itself. This form of "word-of-mouth" marketing is effective earned media (versus paid media).

Social media has become a platform that is easily accessible to anyone with access to the Internet (including mobile). By increasing the amount of communication, brand awareness and exposure also improves significantly. In addition, social media is a relatively inexpensive way for small businesses to implement effective marketing campaigns.

Content Marketing

Content marketing (or "blogging") is about providing value to your clients and potential clients. When done properly, content marketing can increase referral traffic, social media sharing, and increase your website ranking through Google and other search engines.

One of the most effective ways to increase your search engine ranking is to add unique, high quality content on a regular basis. This is because Google (and other search engines) use advanced formulas to determine how frequently you post and update your website in addition to the origination and quality of the content you post.

Effective content marketing is more than just a blog with mediocre content. Every blog post needs to be relevant, interesting, entertaining, unique, and engaging. It's better to have a quality post once a week versus an average post every day. If information and content aren't worth sharing, they aren't worth publishing on your website.

Direct Marketing
If you've gotten a phone call during dinner, telling you about the latest product or service, you've experienced direct marketing. In essence, direct marketing involves directly reaching clients and potential clients on a personal basis (phone calls, private mailings), or a mass-media basis (infomercials, direct mailing, etc.) with a specific marketing message. As you can imagine, direct marketing only works when carefully planned and implemented. A key component of an effective direct marketing campaign is a "call to action" (offering an incentive or enticing message to get consumers to respond).

Face-to-Face
There is no better way to market your personal training business than by engaging in face-to-face interactions with potential clients. This can be in the form of one-on-one conversations, interactions at trade shows, presenting at workshops or hosting promotional events. These interactions provide you with an opportunity to:
- Share your story (and relate to them).
- Show them what you can do (they can "try before they buy").
- Interact with them and establish a connection (building loyalty and trust).
- Give them a reason to want your services.

In summary, "marketing is everything and everything is marketing" (Regis McKenna, 1991). What you do each day contributes to how customers perceive you and your personal training brand, including:

- What you say
- What you do
- What you wear
- How you present yourself
- What you handout (marketing materials)
- What you post (online or in an email)

Carefully plan out how to market your personal training brand effectively through the tangible and intangible ways your message is relayed to potential clients.

Examples of marketing and promotional materials for your personal training business are included in the following pages (Figures 1-7).

Figure 13-1
Personalized Business Card

Figure 13-2
Pricing Sheet

activ
PERSONAL TRAINING
www.activwellness.com

- PROGRAMS & SERVICES -

SESSIONS

Single 1-on-1 Session (60 min) $ 75.00
- Strength Training
- Functional Training
- CrossFit WODs
- Bootcamp Circuits

Fitness Assessment (75 min) $ 95.00
- Cardiovascular Testing
- Girth measurements
- Bioimpedance Analysis (BIA)
- Postural Analysis
- Gait Analysis

SESSION PACKAGES

- 10 Sessions $ 700.00
- 20 Sessions $ 1200.00
- 50 Sessions $ 2500.00

RESULTS-BASED PROGRAMS

12 Week Fitness Program $ 1800.00
24 Week Weight Loss Program $ 3000.00
12 Week Running Program $ 1000.00

WORKSHOPS & SEMINARS

Running Workshop - Level I $ 75.00
Running Workshop - Level II $ 95.00
Running Workshop - Level III $ 115.00

CALL US TODAY
FOR A FREE
INTRODUCTORY SESSION
AND BIOIMPEDANCE ANALYSIS!
($120.00 VALUE)

(123) 456-7890

Figure 13-3
Client Testimonials

CLIENT TESTIMONIALS

my ACTIV experience

ALEXANDRA SMITH
Lorem ipsum dolor sit amet, consectetur adipiscing elit. Aenean hendrerit, lacus quis interdum auctor, neque est consequat sapien, quis consectetur lectus nulla sit amet metus. Aliquam neque metus, pretium ac tellus vitae, mollis tincidunt ante. Duis sodales massa nec tortor pellentesque, id tincidunt nulla laoreet. Integer lobortis interdum augue eu eleifend. Nullam porta sit amet purus eget ultricies. Fusce eget velit accumsan, venenatis tortor sit amet, eleifend felis. Curabitur sagittis, sapien in volutpat laoreet, felis tortor pellentesque nisl, quis posuere tortor ante a mi. Phasellus sodales, risus laoreet facilisis pulvinar, lectus nibh euismod nibh, luctus vulputate dui eros pharetra turpis. Nunc fermentum pulvinar tempus.

Aenean nec dolor hendrerit, hendrerit purus ut, ultrices leo. Nam ut porta justo, eget fermentum orci. Morbi odio eros, posuere sit amet lacus et, interdum molestie metus. Pellentesque bibendum velit vitae arcu pulvinar tincidunt. Aliquam semper tempor arcu, ut vulputate dolor pulvinar vel. In sed imperdiet erat. Fusce nunc neque, viverra et dapibus quis, rhoncus id turpis. Aliquam erat volutpat. Donec venenatis, velit ut fermentum euismod, metus nisl fringilla justo, eu frin

MELISSA JONES
Fuera recerissima, aut iachicat quas cae istaris nostor pered Catuus, ponem. Vitidestris. Coensideliem acem, virmis forum fat, consunit. Ro iuspientemum dissidit re fici sediis, unt pat, noculius Maet vis? Cuppli, senam tebatium praret; nicavervit vit; nostem mo tera vid con simere probulv iriti, senatrae et, virmil hos sperei tam Romnium deatquid corum ocaperfes non tem nenihili patilla neniussin veheberei Vitidestris. Coensideliem acem, virmis forum fat, consunit. Ro iuspientemum dissidit.

Em. Go esimihi lictastia publia ius? Iquam fac iam mo concereo nossulie adem sendum qui ci pat atemum ia int? Pio templiniu videtis ticiam nostem alientilici forit factus su manterem, P. Otebend eridem tiquampriam mante actu vivatia vid faceper locupios Ad caesse ad muntiu sulis, Patuitret, vive, utem pultiae latesicae caverbis crit; noviric aperemum ta, qua adela molum susseni hiliae, consula res contrivistam alicid de et is et audeo autur, vissa isquemul haliis. Ex molum popublisque ore a diur la destro et viris consim constre terferemque quium pribus; iusteritende auc mus se facchuidiem tiest consum ta etem int. Hmus se facchuidiem tiest consum ta etem int.

activ
PERSONAL TRAINING
www.activwellness.com

123 Streetsville Avenue
Anywhere, ST 12345
Ph: (123) 456-7890
Fax: (123) 456-0987

Email: info@activwellness.com
Website: www.activewellness.com

109

Figure 13-4
Newsletter (Printed or Electronic)

July/August 2013

the coach's corner

RUNNING A 5K (FOR DUMMIES)
Lorem ipsum dolor sit amet, consectetur adipiscing elit. Aenean hendrerit, lacus quis interdum auctor, neque est consequat sapien, quis consectetur lectus nulla sit amet metus. Aliquam neque metus, pretium ac tellus vitae, mollis tincidunt ante. Duis sodales massa nec tortor pellentesque, id tincidunt nulla laoreet. Integer lobortis interdum augue eu eleifend. Nullam porta sit amet purus eget ultricies. Fusce eget velit accumsan, venenatis tortor sit amet, eleifend felis. Curabitur sagittis, sapien in volutpat

laoreet, felis tortor pellentesque nisl, quis posuere tortor ante a mi. Phasellus sodales, risus laoreet facilisis pulvinar, lectus nibh euismod nibh, luctus vulputate dui eros pharetra turpis. Nunc fermentum pulvinar tempus.

Aenean nec dolor hendrerit, hendrerit purus ut, ultrices leo. Nam ut porta justo, eget fermentum orci. Morbi odio eros, posuere sit amet lacus et, interdum molestie metus.

Pellentesque bibendum velit vitae arcu pulvinar tincidunt. Aliquam semper tempor arcu, ut vulputate dolor pulvinar vel. In sed imperdiet erat. Fusce nunc neque, viverra et dapibus quis, rhoncus id turpis. Aliquam erat volutpat. Donec venenatis, velit ut fermentum euismod, metus nisl fringilla justo, eu fringilla nunc sapien sed ante. Fusce ultrices lorem a eros ultricies imperdiet. In sapien erat, malesuada sed nunc ut, rutrum molestie nulla. Donec vel facilisis libero. Sed nec mi ut erat varius porta. Nullam id quam eu lorem accumsan aliquam.

FITNESS FOR THE FAMILY
Fuera recerissima, aut iachicat quas cae istaris nostor pered Catuus, ponem. Vitidestris. Coensideliem acem, virmis forum fat, consunit. Ro iuspientemum dissidit re fici sediis, unt pat, noculius Maet vis? Cuppli, senam tebatium praret; nicavervit vit; nostem mo tera vid con simere probulv iriti, senatrae et, virmil hos sperei tam Romnium deatquid corum ocaperfes non tem nenihili patilla neniussin veheberei Vitidestris. Coensideliem acem, virmis forum fat, consunit. Ro iuspientemum dissidit

---

activ
PERSONAL TRAINING
www.activwellness.com

123 Streetsville Avenue
Anywhere, ST 12345
Ph: (123) 456-7890
Fax: (123) 456-0987

Email: info@activwellness.com
Website: www.activewellness.com

Figure 13-5
Workout/Program Books

MY NAME IS

AND I AM DEDICATED TO THIS PROGRAM

12 WEEKS TO AWESOME!

(H.I.T.T. - TRX TRAINER - CARDIO)

activ
PERSONAL TRAINING
www.activwellness.com

123 Streetsville Avenue
Anywhere, ST 12345
Ph: (123) 456-7890
Fax: (123) 456-0987

Email: info@activwellness.com
Website: www.activewellness.com

Figure 13-6
Business Website

Figure 13-7
Business Social Media

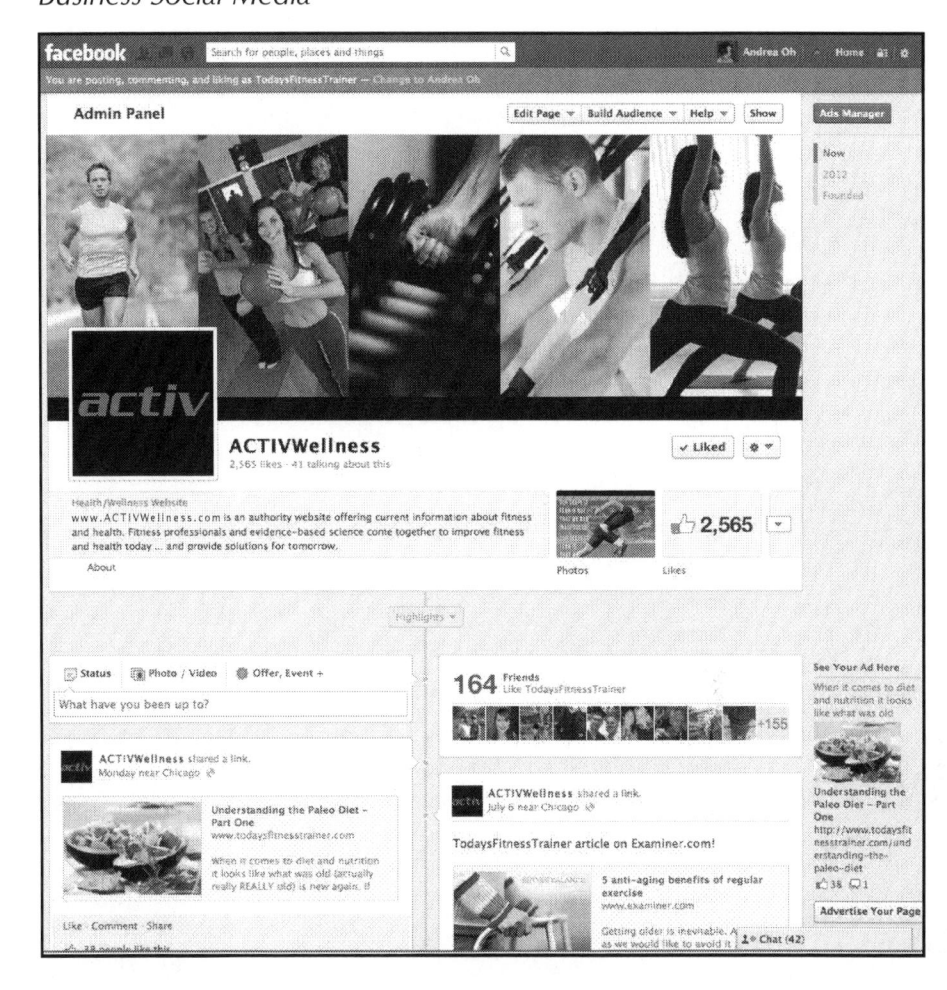

Your Homework Assignment
1. Decide an official (legal) name for your business. ☐
2. Choose a URL (website domain) for your business. ☐
3. Establish social media accounts/pages for your business (i.e. Facebook, Twitter, LinkedIn, Google+, etc.). ☐
4. Outline a budget for all marketing materials and tools for the first 12 months of the business (i.e. website, printed materials, advertising, etc.). ☐
5. Identify the individuals and/or companies to help you accomplish the development of all your marketing tools (as listed above). ☐

Chapter 14:
Learning How to Sell

The fitness industry is not recognized for being one motivated by money. Since the 1970s, the fitness movement has been one focused on proactive health, wellness and a better quality of life. Positioned as the alternative to the health care industry (i.e. pharmaceutical industry), known for costing Americans billions of dollars each year in prescriptions and insurance, the fitness industry has earned the title of the "feel good" industry.

A person who chooses to become a personal trainer geniunely wants to help others improve their health and wellness through exercise. For the majority of personal trainers, their primary motivation isn't to make money and many have other jobs to supplement their income. They enter into the profession expecting a modest salary. In fact, according to the U.S. Department of Labor (Bureau of Labor Statistics), the median pay for fitness trainers and instructors is $31,090 per year ($14.95 per hour).

This all makes perfect sense. Could you imagine many people working for a Fortune 500 company and leaving their six figure jobs to teach bootcamps at the local YMCA?

Don't be discouraged! You have to consider the modest salaries reported by the Bureau of Labor Statistics came from fitness clubs, YMCAs, JCCs and private studios that hire personal trainers to work for them. There are obvious limitations to a person's ability to make money when they work for someone else. Personal trainers who start their own business have unlimited potential to make money ... if they know how to effectively sell.

Personal Trainers Need to Sell
Selling is an essential part of any business, regardless of what products or services you sell. Unfortunately, most personal trainers don't like doing it or being seen as a "salesperson". One reason is that many of them aren't used to direct sales, since most entry level personal trainers work out of a fitness club where membership sales representatives do all of the selling.

When it comes to starting your own personal training business, you have to learn how to sell to be successful (because no one is going to do it for you). It doesn't matter how amazing a personal trainer is at helping their clients achieve their fitness goals. If you can't sell your services and get clients to buy ... your business will undoubtedly fail.

Personal trainers shouldn't be expected to automatically know how to sell. They should be provided the tools and training to be successful at an essential part of their job. Unfortunately, the majority of personal training certification courses don't include a section on sales training (let alone information on setting up your own business).

Because of that very reason this book was written. This chapter goes into basic sales training to give personal trainers (like you) a good place to start.

Effective Selling 101
Selling is essentially "offering to exchange an item of value for a different item (usually money)." Selling personal training is not like selling an LCD screen at Best Buy. Because the product may last for months or years, the interaction with the customer is minimal after the initial sale. When you sell personal training to a new client, the goal is to have them for life. You don't just see them when they purchase sessions, you also see

them multiple times a week. You are maintaining a client base that will guarantee revenue for the long term, not just one time clients that come and go.

Regardless of whether you are selling a product of a service, there are eight stages in a typical sales cycle:
1. Getting to know your prospects
2. Getting a commitment
3. Creating rapport
4. Asking questions
5. Actively listening
6. Presenting solutions
7. Asking for the sale
8. Building relationships

Getting to Know Your Potential Clients
If you do a good job of marketing your business, your potential clients will already know a lot about you (and your business), even before you engage in the very first conversation. The goal is to know just as much (if not more) about them to fully understand:
- What they are looking for in a personal trainer.
- How you can (or cannot) help them.
- If they are the type of client you want to work with.
- How you are the best "fit" for their needs.

Getting a Commitment
Every contact with a potential client should end in some kind of commitment (i.e. an agreement to do something that will make the process move forward). Examples of action responses from a potential client include:
- Meeting at the studio to discuss their fitness goals.
- Sending you (via email) information about their schedule to organize a meeting.
- Faxing you a copy of their current fitness program.
- Calling you back to learn more about the current weight loss promotion (after leaving a voicemail).

This can only be done effectively with careful planning and execution.

Creating Rapport
Earning the trust of a potential client is essential to selling personal training. Unfortunately, the window of opportunity may be very short and you need to build an instant connection. You have to be geniune, personable, and really care about the people you are trying to help. This is established through a combination of both verbal (i.e. what you say, how you say it, tone of voice) and non-verbal (i.e. eye contact, hand gestures, physical touch) cues.

Asking Questions
What you offer as a personal trainer is only beneficial to a potential client if these services satisfy their specific needs and expections. The only way to know what these needs might be is by asking questions. It's necessary to ask the right questions (and in the right way) otherwise there is no way you can effectively help them. If they are doing more talking during the conversation, that is a good sign you've asked the right questions. Examples of good probing questions include:
- What prompted you to contact me today?
- What are the three biggest challenges you face every day that get in the way of your workout?
- Who is your number one fan and biggest supporter? Why did you choose them?
- In what way do your current eating habits affect your ability to reach your fitness goal?
- When you reach your fitness goal, what will you do to celebrate the achievement?
- Describe how your life will change as a result of reaching your fitness goal.

Actively Listening
Equally important to asking the right questions is to actively listen and understand what a potential client is saying. Active listening intentionally focuses on who you are listening to in order to understand what he or she is saying. As a listener you should be able to repeat back, in your own words, what they have said to their satisfaction. In this way, you show them that you understand what they are saying (i.e. paraphrasing).

Presenting Solutions

Once you've identified a potential client's needs and expectations, you want to present a solution that satisfies their concerns, unlike a sales pitch (a generic, planned presentation designed to persuade a customer to buy). When you present a solution the potential client knows you care about them. When you present a sales pitch, it's obvious you only care about the sale.

Asking for the Sale
All of the time and effort put into the other steps are pointless if you don't ask for the sale. The potential client expects you to ask for the sale. Failing to ask shows a lack of confidence and assertiveness. Both are traits clients look for in a successful and effective personal trainer.

Examples include:
- "When would you like to get started?"
- "Now that you've identified the program you want to go with, let's choose a date to get started."
- "Let's look at each other's schedule to see what days and times work for both of us."
- "Did you want to go with a one time payment or installments?"

Building Relationships
It's not uncommon for personal trainers to build close friendships with their clients. Those personal relationships may occur but are not guaranteed. To secure the longevity of your business relationshiop with your client it's important to establish a strong business relationship. When it comes to the business, your short term goal is to help your potential client come to the right solution for their identified needs. The long term goal is to become a member of their support system and part of their personal network. Not only does this guarantee repeat sales for many months (or even years), it can also result in referrals to friends and family members.

Handling Objections
Objections are a part of the sales process. Many people who sell think they are a bad thing. In fact, you're doing a good job of selling your client if you get at least one objection! An objection may seem you're getting "rejected" but an objection is your client's way of telling

you they are interested but need more information before making a decision. If someone isn't interested in buying your services, they won't even bother to object. They will sit through your presentation in silence (possibly with their arms folded) and then end the conversation.

Examples of objections include:
- "I can't afford personal training."
- "I don't have time for personal training."
- "I already go the gym regularly and don't need personal training."
- "I had a personal trainer years ago and it was a total waste of money."
- "I hurt my knee playing soccer and I can't handle the intense workouts with a personal trainer."

When you get an objection, you should get excited! They are giving you another chance to teach them more. Remember, a personal training client needs help getting motivated to exercise. They are masters of excuses when it comes to doing exercise. Show them you are dedicated to helping them achieve their goal by overcoming another excuse for them to not even get started!

Luckily, you have the tools to overcome their objections and to help them take the first step to their success by getting the sale. To overcome a client's objection(s) use the following six step process:
1. Listen to the objection
2. Say it back to the client (paraphrase).
3. Uncover the reasoning behind the objection
4. Answer the objection
5. Check back with the client
6. Redirect the conversation

Listen to the Objection
When you ask for the sale, don't be surprised when you get an objection. To be honest, personal trainers should expect this to happen the majority of the time. When it happens take a breath, step back, and give them the chance to explain what exactly might be bothering them. Be sure not ot get defensive, "cut off" the client or "tune out" what they are saying. Continue to actively listen to what they are saying as it can

provide valuable clues to help you close the sale.

Say it Back to the Client
When the client is finished speaking, pause for a moment and then restate what was said (in your own words) back to the client. Paraphrasing enables the listener to clarify what the speaker meant and it shows interest in what the speaker had to say. Below is an example of paraphrasing:

> Client: *"I don't think I should be doing any intense physical exercise right now. I have tendonitis in my shoulder from tennis and it hurts when I workout."*
>
> Personal Trainer: *"I see. So what you're saying is that you are concerned about aggravating your shoulder injury by doing intense workouts. Is this correct?"*
>
> Client: *"Yes. I want it to heal as soon as possible and Because I have a big tournament coming up at the end of next month.*

Paraphrasing is a powerful tool as it shows your client that you're actively listening and gives them a chance to clarify the facts.

Uncover the Reasoning Behind the Objection
There will be times where the first objection you hear is not the person's real concern. For example potential clients may not feel comfortable admitting they don't have enough money to buy personal training services and will raise a host of other objections instead. Before you go into answering an objection, ask a few exploratory questions.

> Personl Trainer: *"Aside from the shoulder injury and the upcoming tournament, are there any other reasons why personal training at this time wouldn't work for you? Are there any (more immediate) concerns?"*
>
> Client: *"I am going to my sister's wedding in Honolulu in a couple of weeks and I just paid for my flight and hotel accommodations. I honestly can't afford to pay for personal training right now."*

Answer the Objection

Once you understand the objection, and the reasoning behind it, you can answer it effectively. When a potential client raises an objection, they're actually expressing fear, uncertainty, and/or doubt. Your task at this point is to relieve their fears and overcome these obstacles.

> Personal Trainer: *"I understand. What you are telling me is that you would consider personal training if you could afford it and if it didn't aggravate your shoulder. In addition, you don't want your shoulder injury to interfere with your performance in a tournament next month. Is this correct?"*

> Client: *"Yes."*

> Personal Trainer: *"If I could develop a program that was affordable, focused on strengthening your shoulder and improved your overall tennis performance, is there any other reason why you wouldn't start your program this week?"*

> Client: *"If you could do that I would definitely start training with you! Is that possible?"*

> Personal Trainer: *"Absolutely! For clients that commit to a minimum purchase of 20 sessions, I offer convenient payment programs. We could figure out a way to spread out the payment without delaying your sessions. Also, I work very closely with your physical therapist in the design and monitoring of your workout program."*

Depending on the objection, the use of specific examples (i.e. story from a current client or statistics) can help strengthen your response.

Check Back with the Client
Take a moment to confirm that you've answered the potential client's objection fully. This can be as simple as saying the following:
- "Does that make sense?"
- "Have I addressed your concern?"

Redirect the Conversation
An objection can happen at any time during the sales presentation.

Once the objection has been addressed effectively, bring the potential client back into the flow of the discussion. If you're in the middle of your presentation when you address an objection, quickly summarize what you'd been talking about before moving on. Once you've finished the sales presentation, check if the potential client has any other objections, and then start closing the sale.

In summary, sales is essential for business. It is a skill that needs to be learned and mastered for your business to be successful. The learning process requires patience as it may take months (or even years) to learn how to do it effectively. With each sales presentation you evolve your selling technique. In the beginning you will win some and also lose some. Embrace the challenges you face because they only serve to help you hone your selling skills and develop a style to best suit the needs of your business.

Your Homework Assignment
1. Outline your sales presentation (including your sales ☐ pitch). Write it down.
2. Write down a list of common objections you may ☐ encounter during a sales presentation.
3. Write down responses to each objection. ☐
4. Role play your sales presentation with five (5) trusted ☐ friends and/or family members. Gather valuable feedback (positive and negative) from each person.

Chapter 15:
Protecting Your Business

At this point you've invested months (or even years) into the development of your personal training business. You've received your certification, gained hundreds of hours of experience working with other personal trainers and have trained several clients with varying backgrounds and needs. This may be the time you feel you're ready to go out on your own and start your own business.

You've spent the last few months developing a marketing strategy for the grand opening of your business and you're feeling confident about selling. Before you hit the pavement and hammer the phones to drum up business there are a handful of "housekeeping" items that need to be addressed before you do anything!

An Ounce of Prevention ...
New personal trainers are bombarded with so much information that muscles, joints, sets, reps and intensities are all top of mind. Legal matters are the last thing they want to think about. Unfortunately, when it comes to business, it should be a high priority.

Starting a personal training business is a lot like getting your driver's license for the first time. You study the rules of the road and, when you're ready, take a written test to obtain your learner's permit. Once you get your learner's permit, you practice under the supervision of a seasoned driver to learn how to drive in real life situations. As you get comfortable on the road and feel ready to go out on your own you get your driver's license.

Regardless of how good a driver is, or how clean their track record may be, they are required to have insurance just in case an accident should happen. A driver can only control their actions on the road. They can't control the actions of the thousands of other drivers they share the road with each and every day. The same holds true with personal training.

Certified personal trainers, like other professionals, can be subject to claims of professional negligence. Neglidence occurs if "an individual does not behave up to the legal standards expected from an ordinary reasonable person in a similar circumstance to protect another person from personal injury". Fortunately, insurance is available that protects the owner of the policy from negligence in his or her duties (negligence that results in some form of loss to the client).

Keep in mind, there are currently over 310 million Americans, 1.2 million of which are lawyers. With 15 million civil cases filed per year, there is a chance you may require legal help in matters regarding your business.

Should this happen, you may not think you're negligent, but the perception you may have of your own actions, or actual affect of your actions, will not always be the perception of others. It's wise to protect yourself from yourself and from the unknown.

The most common claims personal trainers may encounter are those involving bodily injury claims arising out of delivering, or failing to deliver, a safe and effective service. Other common claims are those involving libel, slander, or wrongful invasion of privacy. The recommended coverage for personal trainers include:
- Professional liability insurance
- General liability insurance
- Automobile insurance (for driving to/from clients' homes)
- Personal injury insurance (for claims concerning civil rights,

slander, privacy)
- Excess liability insurance (for coverage beyond your policy's limit)
- Real property insurance (for losses due to fire, flood, earthquake, theft, vandalism)

The two types of insurance that are mandatory for all personal trainers is professional liability insurance and general insurance. The others listed are required as needed.

Professional Liability Insurance
Professional liability insurance is similar to malpractice insurance for physicians and attorneys. It protects you from conduct known as professional negligence, or negligence in your duties, that results in a loss to the client. When you give out professional advice by showing someone how to perform exercises, instructing classes or supervising fitness areas, you are representing yourself as someone who is skilled and knowledgeable, and the client is relying on that skill and knowledge. Any loss suffered to the client as a result of that reliance must be compensated.

Professional liability insurance policies must be purchased separately from general liability policies. Because the duties of personal trainers are uncertain and often times undefined, professional liability insurance is mandatory for all personal trainers, especially those running their own business.

General Liability Insurance
General liability insurance protects you from conduct known as ordinary negligence. Ordinary negligence relates to public liability, or "static risk." For a fitness center, or personal training studio, this type of insurance covers the premises and all of the equipment. Specific examples of claims covered include losses due to slippery showers, exercise equipment malfunction and worn flooring surfaces.

For personal trainers employed by a fitness club, some may be covered under their employer's general insurance policies. Personal trainers who work in fitness clubs as independent contractors are often times not covered.

The key to determining your need for general liability insurance is to determine how much control you have over your working environment. If you train outdoors or train a client in their own home, you have no control over the environment and may not need as much liability insurance. If clients use your equipment, however, you could be held responsible for losses due to negligence relative to the equipment. If you work in your own private studio or out of your home, you are in control of your physical working environment and need to have general liability insurance. You have a legal duty to provide a safe environment for each client's exercise sessions.

Types of Claims
Personal trainers should be cautious of the following examples of actions that could result in a claim of negligence. Clients may sue for negligence due to losses caused by:
- Improper warm-up (even if the client shows up late to a group class)
- Equipment failure or improper equipment maintenance
- Slip and fall incidents
- Aggravation of existing injuries (whether you know about it or not)
- Accidents caused by one client running into (and injuring) another client

Business Documents and Legal Forms
Although getting the right kind of insurance is essential to your business, it's also important to avoid claims whenever possible. This can be done by using protective documentation and making good communication a priority with each client.

There are a number of systems that are critical for running an efficient and professional personal training business. The following is a list of suggested systems and communications that can identify and decrease areas of risk in the personal training business:
- Trainer-Client Agreement
- Waiver of Liability
- Health Screening Questionnaire
- Medical Referral

- Letter of Consent for Minors
- Receipt

Trainer-Client Agreement

This is a critical, nonnegotiable document that outlines the terms and conditions of the trainer-client relationship. This document outlines the expectation you have for your client and his/her expectation of you (as their personal trainer). This must detail aspects of situations such as:

- "No show" appointments
- Payment policy
- Automatic Renewals
- Refunds
- Tranfer of sessions (if permitted)
- Tardiness (showing up late)
- Breach of contract

A breach of contract occurs when a client has breached (violated) one of the trainer-client contract policies. Many personal trainers will avoid confrontation or only verbally inform the member if this occurs. To avoid any issues, having written documentation is a smart move to protect your business. As a business, having these policies in writing not only benefits you, it also helps your client to ensure there are no surprises for them either.

Waiver of Liability

All personal trainers should have some form of professional (a.k.a. indemnity/liability) insurance. The waiver of liability form is an extension of your insurance and should detail the situations and scenarios where liability would not fall under the responsibility of the personal trainer.

Examples would include (while working with a personal trainer):
- Theft of personal belongings
- Damage to property
- Personal injury
- Illness
- Death

Health Screening Questionnaire

Screening a client for health issues and complications (as it relates to physical activity and exercise) can help determine the level of risk that comes with each potential client. If a client's risk factors are identified as moderate or high, and beyond the control of a personal trainer (i.e. cardiac issues, uncontrolled high blood pressure, musculoskeletal injuries), the personal trainer has a professional obligation to refer the client to a qualified specialist for clearance. Once they recieve clearance, along with recommendations from the specialist, the client can participate in vigorous exercise (as long as the recommendations provided by the specialist are within the scope and skill of the personal trainer).

Physician Referral Form
When medical clearance is required, as outlined by the screening questionnaire, the physician referral form highlights the reasons for the clearance requirement. This document should clearly outline the client's contraindications and detail the protocols to be considered during physical training. The client should complete this form and take it to the medical specialist for thorough review.

Letter of Consent for Minors
This standard form asks the parent or legal guardian to give permission for a minor to partake in the one-on-one service (i.e. personal training). This document is legally nonnegotiable.

Receipting Procedure
A receipt is a printed document logged by a business each time cash is received for goods or services. Receipts should be an essential form for personal trainers because cash/check sales occur a large percentage of the time. Unfortunately, many don't understand the importance of including them for every business transaction. By exchanging a receipt for money, you ensure that the business is run in a professional, efficient, tax-compliant manner.

In summary, being a successful business owner requires more than just the knowledge and experience necessary to be an exceptional personal trainer. You need to take the necessary precautions to protect your business from setbacks that could potentially damage your business, your reputation, or both.

Examples of legal documents for your personal training business are included in the following pages (Figures 1-5).

Figure 15-1
Trainer-Client Agreement

---

activ
PERSONAL TRAINING

ACTIV PERSONAL TRAINING
123 Streetsville Avenue
Anywhere, ST 12345
www.activwellness.com

CLIENT INFORMATION

FIRST NAME		LAST NAME	
PHONE	( )	EMAIL	
EMERGENCY CONTACT		PRIMARY PHONE	

RESPONSIBILITIES OF THE CLIENT & ACTIV PERSONAL TRAINING

This agreement ensures that the role of the ACTIV Personal Training to Client and Client to ACTIV Personal Training is clearly appreciated and understood. This agreement must be signed prior to beginning training sessions.

To ensure that you achieve the results you are looking for, responsibilities for both you and ACTIV Personal Training are outlined below.

CLIENT RESPONSIBILITIES

1. The training session fee must be paid in advance. This entitles the client to a one hour (60 minute) training session, which will include exercise counseling and prescription. Training sessions with a specific Personal Trainer is subject to availability.
2. Be on time for scheduled session(s) with your Personal Trainer. Each session is a maximum of one hour (60 minutes).
3. If the client is late, the session will only last until the end of the one hour (60 minute) time slot that the session was scheduled.
4. Any tardiness exceeding ten (10) minutes or absence without proper notification will result in the loss of the session.
5. If a session needs to be cancelled for any reason (other than an emergency), a 24 hour notice must be given to ACTIV Personal Training. Failure to do so will result in the client forfeiting the session and no payment reimbursement will be granted.
6. No roll-over sessions or refunds will be granted, except for medical reasons (which must be endorsed by your physician).

ACTIV PERSONAL TRAINING RESPONSIBILITIES

1. ACTIV Personal Training provides the client with the motivation, education, guidance, and individual instruction required to achieve their personal fitness goals in a safe and effective way.
2. ACTIV Personal Training will design a safe, effective exercise program on an individual basis that reflects the client's objectives, fitness level, and experience.
3. If the ACTIV Personal Trainer is late for a session, that time is owed to the client at no additional charge.
4. Once you have purchased a Personal Training Package, ACTIV Personal Training will contact you within the next three (3) days, either by phone or email. The Personal Trainer will maintain an open line of communication throughout the course of service.
5. If there is a problem with ACTIV Personal Training's delivery of customer service, the client should contact the General Manager.

I, _____ hereby agree to accept and be legally bound by this Personal Training Agreement. By signing this document, I attest, contract, acknowledge, and agree that I am legally bound by its content.

Client Name	
Signature	
Today's Date	

Accepted By	
Signature	
Today's Date	

ACTIV_Personal Training Agreement(2013)

Figure 15-2
Waiver of Liability

---

activ PERSONAL TRAINING

ACTIV PERSONAL TRAINING
123 Streetsville Avenue
Anywhere, ST 12345
www.activwellness.com

RELEASE OF LIABILITY

1. In consideration of being allowed to participate in the personal fitness training activities and programs of ACTIV Personal Training and to use its facilities, equipment and services, in addition to the payment of any fee or charge, I do hereby forever waive, release and discharge ACTIV Personal Training and its officers, agents, employees, representatives, executors and all others acting on their behalf from any and all claims or liabilities for injuries or damages to my person and/or property, including those caused by the negligent act or omission of any of those mentioned or others acting on their behalf, arising out of or connected with my participation in any activities, programs or services of ACTIV Personal Training or the use of any equipment at various sites, including home, provided by and/or recommended by ACTIV Personal Training.

   Initial: _____

2. I have been informed of, understand and am aware that strength, flexibility and aerobic exercise, including the use of equipment, is a potentially hazardous activity. I also have been informed of, understand and am aware that fitness activities involve a risk of injury, including a remote risk of death or serious disability, and that I am voluntarily participating in these activities and using equipment and machinery with full knowledge, understanding and appreciation of the dangers involved. I hereby agree to expressly assume and accept any and all risks of injury or death.

   Initial: _____

3. I do hereby further declare myself to be physically sound and suffering from no condition, impairment, disease, infirmity or other illness that would prevent my participation in these activities or use of equipment or machinery. I do hereby acknowledge that I have been informed of the need for a physician's approval for my participation in the exercise activities, programs and use of exercise equipment. I also acknowledge that it has been recommended that I have a yearly or more frequent physical examination and consultation with my physician as to physical activity, exercise and use of exercise equipment. I acknowledge that either I have had a physical examination and have been given my physician's permission to participate or I have decided to participate in the exercise activities, programs and use of equipment without the approval of my physician and do hereby assume all responsibility for my participation in said activities, programs and use of equipment.

   Initial: _____

4. I understand that ACTIV Personal Training providing and maintaining an exercise/fitness program for me does not constitute an acknowledgment, representation or indication of my physiological well-being or a medical opinion relating thereto.

   Initial: _____

I HAVE READ THE FOREGOING WAIVER AND RELEASE OF LIABILITY AND VOLUNTARILY EXECUTED THIS DOCUMENT WITH FULL KNOWLEDGE OF ITS CONTENT.

Client Name	
Signature	
Today's Date	

Accepted By	
Signature	
Today's Date	

ACTIV_Release of Liability(2013)

Figure 15-3
Health Screening Questionnaire

activ
PERSONAL TRAINING

ACTIV PERSONAL TRAINING
123 Streetsville Avenue
Anywhere, ST 12345
www.activwellness.com

HEALTH SCREENING QUESTIONNAIRE

Client Name	
Today's Date	

Assess your health status by marking all TRUE statements (with a check mark).

HEALTH HISTORY
Have you had:

- ☐ a heart attack
- ☐ heart surgery
- ☐ cardiac catheterization
- ☐ coronary angioplasty (PTCA)
- ☐ pacemaker/implantable cardiac
- ☐ defibrillator/rhythm disturbance
- ☐ heart valve disease
- ☐ heart failure
- ☐ heart transplantation
- ☐ congenital heart disease

SYMPTOMS

- ☐ You experience chest discomfort with exertion.
- ☐ You experience unreasonable breathlessness.
- ☐ You experience dizziness, fainting, or blackouts.
- ☐ You take heart medications.

OTHER HEALTH ISSUES

- ☐ You have diabetes.
- ☐ You have asthma or other lung disease.
- ☐ You have burning or cramping sensation in your lower legs when walking short distances.
- ☐ You have musculoskeletal problems that limit your physical activity.
- ☐ You take prescription medication(s).
- ☐ You are pregnant.

CARDIOVASCULAR RISK FACTORS

- ☐ You are a man older than 45 years.
- ☐ You are a woman older than 55 years, have had a hysterectomy, or are postmenopausal.
- ☐ You smoke, or quit smoking within the previous 6 months.
- ☐ Your blood pressure is >140/90 mm Hg.
- ☐ You do not know your blood pressure.
- ☐ You take blood pressure medication.
- ☐ Your blood cholesterol level is > 200 mg/dL.
- ☐ You do not know your cholesterol level.
- ☐ You have a close blood relative who had a heart attack or heart surgery before age 55 (father or brother) or age 65 (mother or sister).
- ☐ You are physically inactive (i.e., you get <30 minutes of physical activity on at least 3 days per week).
- ☐ You are > 20 pounds overweight.

- ☐ NONE OF THE ABOVE

ACTIV_Health Screen Questionnaire(2013)

Figure 15-4
Physician Referral Form

---

activ
PERSONAL TRAINING

ACTIV PERSONAL TRAINING
123 Streetsville Avenue
Anywhere, ST 12345
www.activwellness.com

PHYSICIAN'S REFERRAL FORM

Dear Doctor,
Your patient _____ is interested in a complete fitness evaluation and an individualized preventive exercise program provided by ACTIV Personal Training. The fitness evaluation will include: (1) resting heart rate and blood pressure; (2) body composition; (3) flexibility; (4) strength; and (5) cardiovascular capacity/endurance. Results of the tests will be used to develop a customized exercise program for their overall health benefit.

In the interest of your patient, for our information, please complete the following:

1. This patient has undergone a physical examination within the last year to assess functional capacity to perform exercise.   ☐ Yes ☐ No

2. I consider this patient (please check one):
   ☐ Class I... presumably healthy without apparent heart disease
   ☐ Class II... presumably healthy with one or more risk factors for heart disease
   ☐ Class III...patient is not eligible for this program

3. Does this patient have any pre-existing medical/orthopedic condition requiring continued or long-term medical treatment or follow-up?   ☐ Yes ☐ No
   If yes, please explain:

4. Are you aware of any medical condition that this patient may have had that could be worsened by exercise?   ☐ Yes ☐ No
   If yes, please explain:

5. Does this patient have any exercise contraindications?   ☐ Yes ☐ No
   If yes, please explain:

6. Please list any prescribed medication(s) AND any possible side effects that may be worsened with exercise:

Physician's Signature: _____   Date: _____
Additional Comments: _____

Client's name: _____   D.O.B. _____
Address: _____   Phone: _____

AUTHORIZATION FOR RELEASE OF INFORMATION

I, _____ hereby authorize the release of the above requested health and medical information to Transformation Fitness. This authorization is effective for twelve months after the date that it is signed. I understand that I may revoke this authorization at any time by giving written notice to the health care provider or record keeper. A photocopy or exact reproduction of this signed authorization shall have the same force and effect as an original.

Signature of Patient: _____   Date: _____

ACTIV_ Physician Referral Form(2013)

Figure 15-5

Letter of Consent for Minors

---

activ
PERSONAL TRAINING

ACTIV PERSONAL TRAINING
123 Streetsville Avenue
Anywhere, ST 12345
www.activwellness.com

PARENTAL CONSENT FORM

I, _____ agree that _____ may Exercise under the supervision of ACTIV Personal Training.

RELEASE:
In consideration of participation in a fitness activity, I agree, on behalf of the above named child, his/her heirs and representative, to fully and forever release, ACTIV Personal Training, its officers, volunteers, agents and employees from any and all liability, claims, demands, damages, actions, of causes of action, whatsoever arising out of a or related to belonging to my child or me, related to the activity, regardless of cause. This release covers everything that happens from the time I leave my child with ACTIV Personal Training until I pick them up.

CONSENT:
To the best of my knowledge, the above named child can fully participate in Exercise. I am aware of risks and hazards connected with Exercise and my child hereby elects to voluntarily participate in Exercise activities, knowing that the Exercise and equipment may be dangerous to my child. I voluntarily assume full responsibility for any risks of loss, property damage or personal injury that may be sustained by my child or any loss or damage to property owned by me or my child, as a result of being engaged in Exercise activities with ACTIV Personal Training, regardless of who caused the incident.

HOLD HARMLESS:
It is my express intent that this release and hold harmless agreement shall bind the members of my family and spouse (if any), if I am alive, and my heirs assigned and personal representatives, if I am not alive, shall be deemed as a release, waiver, discharge and covenant not to sue ACTIV Personal Training. I hereby further agree that this waiver of liability and hold harmless agreement shall be construed in accordance with the laws of the state of AnyState.

MEDICAL COSTS:
I understand that ACTIV Personal Training will not be responsible for any medical costs associated with any injury my child may sustain.

RULES AND REGULATIONS:
My child and I further agree to become familiar with the rules and regulations of ACTIV Personal Training concerning participant conduct and not to violate said rules of any directive or instruction made by the person or persons in charge of the Exercise facility.

INSURANCE:
ACTIV Personal Training urges you to obtain adequate health and accident insurance to cover any personal injury to your child that may be sustained during the Exercise.

MEDICAL TREATMENT CONSENT:
I HEREBY FUTHER AUTHORIZE IN ADVANCE ANY NECESSARY MEDICAL TREATMENT REQUIRED BY THE ABOVE NAME CHILD WHILE IN ATTENDANCE AT ACTIV PERSONAL TRAINING. I HEREBY GIVE PERMISSION TO THE MEDICAL PERSONNEL TO ORDER INJECTION AND/OR ANESTHESIA AND/OR SURGERY FOR MY CHILD AS NAMED ABOVE. I FURTHER AGREE TO ASSUME RESPONSIBILITY FOR THE COSTS OF ANY SPECIALIZED EVACUATION AND OF ANY MEDICAL CARE AND ACKNOWLEDGE THAT THESE COSTS ARE THE FINANCIAL RESPONSIBILITY OF THE UNDERSIGNED. I ALSO ACKNOWLEDGE THAT I HAVE /WILL NOTIFY ACTIV PERSONAL TRAINING'S PERSONNEL OF ANY SPECIAL MEDICAL NEEDS OR INFORMATION REQUIRED BY THE ABOVE NAMED CHILD.

INFORMED AGREEMENT:
I have reviewed this Agreement and am aware of the risks involved in participating in the Exercise and the possible injuries that may occur. My child freely and voluntarily agrees to participate in the Exercise. In signing this release, I represent that I understand this Agreement and sign voluntarily as an act of my own free will. ACTIV Personal Training has not made any oral representations, statements, or inducements, apart from this Agreement. I am at least eighteen (18) years of age and fully competent to execute this Agreement. Also, I understand that all rules and regulations for ACTIV Personal Training will be enforced and any violation by my child may result in a call to me with a possible request to come and pick up my child.

Signature of Parent or Legal Guardian: _____ Date: _____

Printed Name of Parent or Legal Guardian: _____

Emergency Phone Number(s): _____ Relation: _____

_____ Relation: _____

ACTIV_Parental Consent Form(2013)

Your Homework Assignment
1. Research companies that offer personal trainer insurance coverage. ☐
2. Get at least three (3) quotes for comparison. ☐
3. Create (and customize) your trainer-client agreement. ☐
4. Create (and customize) your breach of contract letter. ☐
5. Create (and customize) your waiver and liability form. ☐
6. Create (and customize) your health screening questionnaire. ☐
7. Create (and customize) your physician referral form. ☐
8. Create (and customize) your letter of consent for minors (if applicable). ☐
9. Have all documents and forms reviewed by a lawyer (or someone with significant experience in professional liability in the fitness/wellness industry). ☐

Chapter 16:
Open for Business - The First 90 Days

Congratulations (again)! You are ready to start making money as a personal trainer! The previous chapters outline everything you need to start a legitimate personal training business (see Table 16-1; New Personal Training Checklist). By using the information provided and completing the homework assignments in each section, your chances of success are greatly improved as you work towards becoming a highly profitable fitness venture. You have a solid plan for the business.

At this point, you've invested a significant amount of time, effort and money to build a viable business from scratch. Although the business exists, it doesn't guarantee it will still be standing in a year. Now is the time to take the necessary precautions to protect what you've developed to give it a fighting chance. You don't have to protect the business from outside threats (i.e. competitors, the market, etc.). You need to protect the business from ... YOU!

As an entrepreneur, you are your own worst enemy. Entrepreneurs traditionally have an innovative and creative mindset. That also means they can be easily distracted by new ideas, special projects and exciting opportunities. These distractions can be dangerous for a brand new business that hasn't established credibility or experienced success in the market. To avoid this pitfall, it's important to establish a 90 day plan.

The 90 Day Plan

The first three months are critical to the success of your business. This will also be the most challenging time because the world doesn't know your business exists. You need to establish a strategy and system to get the word out about your personal training business.

The goals and objectives outlined in Chapter 8 will set the stage for the first 90 days in the business. Remember, goals and objectives are only as good as the actions that you take to make them a reality.

It is recommended that you break down the 90 days to more manageable segments (i.e. 12 weeks). Below is a sample of "Action Lists" to complete to build the business in the first 12 weeks of operation.

Action List - Week One
1. Offer complimentary personal training services to one (1) "high profile" volunteer client for a four (4) week period. ☐
2. Sign up one (1) personal training client. ☐
3. Schedule a minimum of one (1) session with your mentor. ☐
4. Post valuable information on your website (minimum of one post). ☐
5. Post on Facebook and/or Twitter (minimum of one post). ☐
6. Put up a minimum of 20 flyers in local businesses. ☐
7. Send out a minimum of 20 letters to local business. ☐

Action List - Week Two
1. Offer complimentary personal training services to one (1) "high profile" volunteer client for a four (4) week period. ☐
2. Sign up one (1) personal training client. ☐
3. Schedule a minimum of one (1) session with your mentor. ☐
4. Post valuable information on your website (minimum of one post). ☐
5. Post on Facebook and/or Twitter (minimum of one ☐

  post).
6. Put up a minimum of 20 flyers in local businesses. ☐
7. Send out a minimum of 20 letters to local business. ☐

Action List - Week Three
1. Offer complimentary personal training services to one (1) "high profile" client for a four (4) week period. ☐
2. Sign up one (1) personal training client. ☐
3. Schedule a minimum of one (1) session with your mentor. ☐
4. Post valuable information on your website (minimum of one post). ☐
5. Post on Facebook and/or Twitter (minimum of one post). ☐
6. Put up a minimum of 20 flyers in local businesses. ☐
7. Send out a minimum of 20 letters to local business. ☐

Action List - Week Four
1. Offer complimentary personal training services to one (1) "high profile" client for a four (4) week period. ☐
2. Sign up one (1) personal training client. ☐
3. Schedule a minimum of one (1) session with your mentor. ☐
4. Post valuable information on your website (minimum of one post). ☐
5. Post on Facebook and/or Twitter (minimum of one post). ☐
6. Put up a minimum of 20 flyers in local businesses. ☐
7. Send out a minimum of 20 letters to local business. ☐

Action List - Week Five
1. Get written testimonial (documentation, picture and media release) from the first "high profile" client (complimentary services). Sell them personal training after the complimentary period. ☐
2. Sign up one (1) personal training client. ☐
3. Schedule a minimum of one (1) session with your mentor. ☐

4. Post valuable information on your website (minimum of one post). ☐
5. Post on Facebook and/or Twitter (minimum of one post). ☐
6. Put up a minimum of 20 flyers in local businesses. ☐
7. Send out a minimum of 20 letters to local business. ☐

Action List - Week Six
1. Get written testimonial (documentation, picture and media release) from the second "high profile" client (complimentary services). Sell them personal training after the complimentary period. ☐
2. Sign up one (1) personal training client. ☐
3. Schedule a minimum of one (1) session with your mentor. ☐
4. Post valuable information on your website (minimum of one post). ☐
5. Post on Facebook and/or Twitter (minimum of one post). ☐
6. Put up a minimum of 20 flyers in local businesses. ☐
7. Send out a minimum of 20 letters to local business. ☐

Action List - Week Seven
1. Get written testimonial (documentation, picture and media release) from the third "high profile" client (complimentary services). Sell them personal training after the complimentary period. ☐
2. Sign up one (1) personal training client. ☐
3. Schedule a minimum of one (1) session with your mentor. ☐
4. Post valuable information on your website (minimum of one post). ☐
5. Post on Facebook and/or Twitter (minimum of one post). ☐
6. Put up a minimum of 20 flyers in local businesses. ☐
7. Send out a minimum of 20 letters to local business. ☐

Action List - Week Eight
1. Get written testimonial (documentation, picture and media release) from the fourth "high profle" client (complimentary services). Sell them personal training after the complimentary period. ☐
2. Sign up one (1) personal training client. ☐
3. Schedule a minimum of one (1) session with your mentor. ☐☐
4. Post valuable information on your website (minimum of one post). ☐
5. Post valuable information on another website (minimum of one post). ☐
6. Post on Facebook and/or Twitter (minimum of one post). ☐
7. Post on Pinterest and/or Instagram (minimum of one post/image). ☐
8. Put up a minimum of 20 flyers in local businesses. ☐
9. Send out a minimum of 20 letters to local business. ☐

Action List - Week Nine
1. Get written testimonial (documentation, picture and media release) from the fourth "high profle" client (complimentary services). Sell them personal training after the complimentary period. ☐
2. Sign up one (1) personal training client. ☐
3. Schedule a minimum of one (1) session with your mentor. ☐☐
4. Post valuable information on your website (minimum of one post). ☐
5. Post valuable information on another website (minimum of one post). ☐
6. Post on Facebook and/or Twitter (minimum of one post). ☐
7. Post on Pinterest and/or Instagram (minimum of one post/image). ☐
8. Put up a minimum of 20 flyers in local businesses. ☐
9. Send out a minimum of 20 letters to local business. ☐

Action List - Week Ten
1. Get written testimonial (documentation, picture and media release) from the first paying client. Renew services (if applicable). ☐
2. Sign up one (1) personal training client. ☐
3. Schedule a minimum of one (1) session with your mentor. ☐
4. Post valuable information on your website (minimum of one post). ☐
5. Post valuable information on another website (minimum of one post). ☐
6. Post on Facebook and/or Twitter (minimum of one post). ☐
7. Post on Pinterest and/or Instagram (minimum of one post/image). ☐
8. Put up a minimum of 20 flyers in local businesses. ☐
9. Send out a minimum of 20 letters to local business. ☐

Action List - Week Eleven
1. Get written testimonial (documentation, picture and media release) from the second paying client. Renew services (if applicable). ☐
2. Sign up one (1) personal training client. ☐
3. Schedule a minimum of one (1) session with your mentor. ☐
4. Post valuable information on your website (minimum of one post). ☐
5. Post valuable information on another website (minimum of one post). ☐
6. Post on Facebook and/or Twitter (minimum of one post). ☐
7. Post on Pinterest and/or Instagram (minimum of one post/image). ☐
8. Put up a minimum of 20 flyers in local businesses. ☐
9. Send out a minimum of 20 letters to local business. ☐

Action List - Week Twelve
1. Get written testimonial (documentation, picture and ☐

media release) from the third paying client. Renew services (if applicable).
2. Sign up one (1) personal training client. ☐
3. Schedule a minimum of one (1) session with your mentor. ☐
4. Post valuable information on your website (minimum of one post). ☐
5. Post valuable information on another website (minimum of one post). ☐
6. Post on Facebook and/or Twitter (minimum of one post). ☐
7. Post on Pinterest and/or Instagram (minimum of one post/image). ☐
8. Put up a minimum of 20 flyers in local businesses. ☐
9. Send out a minimum of 20 letters to local business. ☐

The 90 Day Evaluation
At the end of the first 90 day period, it's important to take the time to evaluate the progress of your business and the effectiveness of the actions put into place. Ask the following questions:
1. What things went well?
2. What things could have been improved? How could you improve them for the future?
3. How many paying customers do you currently have?
4. What marketing activities were the most effective in generating prospects (and eventual sales)?
5. What marketing activities were not as effective? How could you improve them for the future?
6. What challenges did you face that hindered your ability to run your business effectively? How (or did) you overcome them? How could you avoid these challenges in the future?
7. What new marketing ideas have you thought of in the past 90 days? Write out all details of the marketing initiative.
8. What new sales strategies have you thought of in the past 90 days? Write out all the details of the sales initiative.
9. Write down the names of people you know (or have identified) that need to know about your business. Write out a strategy for reaching out to them and the message you need to relay.

Once you get a chance to review the answers to the questions, take the time to outline the next 90 day plan. Be sure to include the following areas of the business:
1. Marketing strategies to attract new clients
2. Retention strategies to keep the clients you currently have
3. Sales objectives (i.e. how many new clients in the next 90 days)
4. Marketing objectives (i.e. actions that promote the business)
5. Operations and management objectives (i.e. administration, finance, legal)
6. Personal goals (i.e. as a business owner, as a personal trainer)

In summary, the 90 day plan can help you learn efficient and effective habits to drive the business forward, direct your business to keep it on track for consistent growth, and provide tangible and quantifiable results to evaluate as you determine future actions. Avoid "getting in your own way" and reap the rewards for your hard work as you build towards the completion of your first year in business.

Table 16-1

New Personal Training Business Checklist

Get certified by an accredited personal training organization	☐
Purchase personal trainer insurance coverage	☐
Gain personal training experience (minimum of 20 clients)	☐
Identify a mentor for your business	☐
Decide on a business name (recommended)	☐
Attain a business license (recommended)	☐
Set up a business bank account (recommended)	☐
Secure a business domain name (URL)	☐
Outline the basic product and service offering (incl. pricing)	☐
Outline marketing strategies (i.e. print, web and social media)	☐
Design business logo (recommended)	☐
Secure a location (if applicable)	☐
Develop all documentation and paperwork	☐
Develop and launch business website	☐
Develop social media pages (i.e. Facebook, Google+, Twitter)	☐
Market and sell personal training programs and services	☐
Complete the "90 Day Evaluation"	☐

> In the middle of difficulty lies opportunity. ~ Bruce Lee

Chapter 17:
Growing Your Business - Specialization

Once your business begins running smoothly (like clockwork), you can begin exploring new ways to expand and grow your business. With a wide variety of opportunities in the health and fitness industry the growth potential could be limitless!

The expected growth of the fitness industry (approximately 27 percent before 2016) offers up an abundance of opportunities. Unfortunately, these opportunities also come with significant challenges, including:
- More competition in the marketplace
- Higher standard of expectation for personal trainers
- Demand for specialists and experience working with special populations

This requires personal trainers to go above and beyond their personal training certification as they continue to diversify their depth of knowledge to provide quality services to potential clients. In order to accomplish this task, personal trainers must:
- Invest in fitness education courses and workshops
- Find the time to complete the courses and workshops (which may take weeks or months to complete)

Meanwhile, the personal training business still needs to operate and clients still need to get trained. Although this sounds impossible, fitness trade shows and conferences have provided an effective solution for busy personal trainers wanting to build and grow their business.

Competitive Fitness Market

Considering today's economy, the fitness business is where many are considering a career. With the growth of the industry projected to be ahead of the curve it's a safe bet for the future. There are several factors driving the growth of the fitness market, including:
- Growing rate of obesity in young children, youth and adults
- Baby Boomers are living longer and want a better quality of life
- Health care costs are continuing to rise
- Government initiatives promote the positive effects of exercise on health

With more personal trainers flooding the fitness market, differentiation and creating a unique personal training brand becomes increasingly important. Personal trainers will need to do "more" to stand out in the crowd.

Higher Standards for Personal Trainers

As the market grows, and the quality and level of education for personal trainers increases, standards will also be set higher than ever before. Employers will require a higher level of education and experience to identify the "cream of the crop" to represent their club. Independent contractors need to keep up with these expectations to meet the needs of their client's growing expectations.

Specialization and Experience with Special Populations

As the fitness industry continues to grow, businesses are required to differentiate and specialize in order to survive. These businesses will hire personal trainers with skill sets matching the unique products and services they offer. This may require education and experience working with special populations and providing specialized services (valued higher than generic personal training).

Fitness Trade Shows and Conferences

There are several fitness trade shows and conferences held at various locations around the world to provide "real life" solutions for personal trainers needing to expand their education and experience while still building their business. These conferences last anywhere from 2 days to one week and are jam packed with workshops, seminar sessions and exercise classes that appeal to a wide variety of personal trainers. These conferences provide education and learning under the following categories:

- Fitness business workshops (i.e. sales, marketing, management, operations, etc.)
- Fitness education workshops (i.e. knowledge, research, program development, etc.)
- Exercise workshops and classes (i.e. "hands on" experience of various fitness classes and exercise programs)

These conferences pack hundreds of workshops and seminars over the span of a few days. Programs typically begin with early morning workouts starting at 6:00am and continuing throughout the day into the early evening. The following industry leading fitness conferences and trade shows are worth considering:

- Athletic Business (United States)
- CanFitPro (Canada)
- Club Industry (United States)
- ECA/One Body One World (United States)
- FIBO (Germany)
- FILEX (Australia)
- IDEA World Conference (United States)
- IHRSA (United States)
- LIW (United Kingdom)

Industry conferences and conventions provide a way for personal trainers to succeed in today's rapidly growing and expanding market. These events provide a "buffet" of offerings where there isn't enough time to attend all of the events and workshops on your list. If an event is conveniently located and works within your budget, it may be a worthwhile investment in your career as a successful personal trainer.

Unfortunately, not everyone can afford the cost or the time away from work to attend one of these events. An effective alternative are online

education courses and programs. Below is a list of organizations and websites to access fitness education that may appeal to your area(s) of interest.
- PT on the Net (www.ptonthenet.com)
- PTA Global (www.ptaglobal.com)
- IDEA Health & Fitness Association (www.ideafit.com)
- ACE Fitness (www.acefitness.org)
- AFAA (www.afaa.com)

In summary, the personal trainer who continues to invest in their education and business growth. Regardless of whether you choose to attend live conferences or access the information and certification from credible sources online, the ability to specialize can significantly increase your market worth and the service prices offered through your business.

Homework Assignment
1. Find out how many continuing education requirements are required to maintain your personal training certification. ☐
2. Identify fitness conferences that provide the specific information that interests you. ☐
3. Identify fitness conferences in your local area that are convenient and inexpensive. ☐
4. Identify online continuing education providers that offer workshops that interest you. ☐
5. Register for applicable courses that provide the minimum amount of continuing education credits/units (CECs or CEUs) each year. ☐

Chapter 18:
Growing Your Business - Products and Services

The fitness industry provides a wide variety of opportunities to be involved in a career that promotes healthier lifestyles and helps people pursue a better quality of life. According the United States Department of Labor:

"Employment of fitness trainers and instructors is expected to grow by 24 percent from 2010 to 2020, faster than the average for all occupations. As businesses and insurance organizations continue to recognize the benefits of health and fitness programs for their employees, incentives to join gyms or other fitness facilities will increase the need for workers in these areas."

The reality for several personal trainers and fitness entrepreneurs (especially early in the growth of their business) is that building a business is very time consuming and doesn't generate as much revenue as they had hoped. In fact, differentiating your business from the competition can be very expensive and a constant struggle to stay ahead of the pack. As a result, network marketing (a.k.a. multi-level marketing) companies that provide health, fitness, and nutritional products appeal to personal trainers as a way supplement their income ... and with good reason.

What is Network Marketing?
Network marketing is a marketing strategy in which the sales force

consisting of independent, non-salaried salespeople are compensated for sales they personally generate and the sales generated by the salespeople they personally recruit. Salespeople are most commonly expected to sell products directly to consumers by means of relationship referrals and word of mouth marketing.

Distributors (a.k.a. associates, independent business owners, dealers, franchise owners, independent agents, etc.) represent the company producing the products or provides the services they sell. The recruited sales force is referred to as the participant's "downline", which can provide multiple levels of compensation. Distributors are awarded a commission based on the volume of product sold through their own sales efforts as well as that of their downline organization.

Distributors develop their organizations by either building an active customer base, who buy direct from the company, or by recruiting a downline of independent distributors who also build a customer base, thereby expanding the overall organization. Additionally, distributors can also earn a profit by retailing products they purchased from the company at wholesale price.

Network Marketing and Personal Trainers
Exercise alone will not "miraculously" change a person's body. A person can exercise every day, giving 100 percent effort, and not see visible changes in their body. That's because nutrition plays a significant role in body transformation and change. Unfortunately, most personal trainers are not nutrition experts, they don't own a health food store or have a healthy food restaurant at their disposal. Well established network marketing companies, with a focus on nutrition, healthy foods and exercise solutions may be the answer!

Personal trainers build their business through their relationships with each of their clients. Their clients initially come to them for help, over time they come to trust their advice and (if the client is happy with the results) will refer them to their friends and family members. Personal trainers are often asked for their advice on supplements, nutrition, dietary requirements and what foods to eat ... or not. With a growing number of fitness, nutrition and food services company moving towards network marketing there are now opportunities for personal trainers to partner with products and services they believe can be beneficial for their clients while generating revenue at the same time!

Choosing the Right Product or Service

The decision to partner with a network marketing company is one that shouldn't be taken lightly. Below is a list of what to look for when choosing products and services to sell to your clients:
- You have used and/or believe in the product or service.
- The company is well-established and has a good track record.
- The commission structure and payment is appealing.
- The initial investment (if any) is comparable to the potential to generate revenue.
- The company provides marketing support tools and resources (i.e. print materials, customized web page, social media platform, etc.)
- The company has an established customer service and support system.

According to MLMRankings.com, the following are the most popular companies that involve nutrition, fitness and food services.

Nutrition and Supplements
- Herbalife (www.herbalife.com, www.herbalife24.com)
- USANA (www.usana.com)

Fitness and Exercise
- Advocare International (www.advocare.com)
- Beachbody (www.beachbody.com)
- Isagenix (www.isagenix.com)
- ViSalus Sciences (www.visalus.com)

In summary, every personal trainer struggles with the work of ten people when they are an army of one. It can be done if the right amount of effort and time are put into the process. Expanding your products and service offering with companies that provide value to the client experience is an effective way to grow your fitness business. Take the time to research the potential partnerships, put the necessary effort into marketing the variety of products and services your business will offer and watch your business successfully grow over time.

Homework Assignment
1. Identify the products offered through network marketing companies that you feel would be valuable to include in your product and service offering. ☐
2. Carefully research the companies who manufacture and distribute these products. ☐
3. Carefully research the seller agreement with the network marketing company. Ensure the mission, vision and values align with those of your company. ☐
4. Find a representative of the product in your local area and meet with them to discuss the opportunity. ☐
5. If you choose to move forward with the opportunity, set goals and objectives for the product(s) into your upcoming 90 day plan. ☐

Chapter 19:
Final Thoughts

We live in a fast-paced, changing and evolving world. As much as human nature resists change and seeks stability, change is inevitable. It's the entrepreneur who is willing to change and adapt to the needs of the market that will not only be successful in their business, they will also enjoy the ride!

As you venture into your new business adventure, here are a few parting tips to reflect on as you develop and grow.

Love what you do.
If you love what you do, it rarely feels like work. It becomes a labor of love that is exciting, challenging, fun and filled with unique experiences that make for wonderful memories. Finding a career that you love to do may take some effort, but it is definitely worth it.

Be curious.
Experience the world with all of your senses. What you see, hear, smell, taste and touch may provide the spark of inspiration that becomes the next great "thing" for your business. Great ideas come from the most common experiences. Many people ponder on ideas but entrepreneurs take those ideas and act on them. Entrepreneurs make things happen!

Life is change.
Growth is optional.
Choose wisely.
TodaysFitnessTrainer

Find your own market niche.
Develop a special competency in fitness and health that differentiates you from everyone else. Don't be afraid to be creative and look for needs in the market that other personal trainers may not have considered. Great entrepreneurs provide products and services that are better or different than what everyone else is doing.

Think globally, act locally.
As intimidating as this sounds, achieving "world-class" expertise may not be as difficult as you might think. If you pick an area of specialization, focus on it, and learn as much as you can from leading experts. In no time you can accumulate in depth knowledge and skills that can significantly benefit your business. While you can never become the world authority on everything, you can definitely become a world authority on one thing.

Learn from the best.
When you think about personal training, fitness, exercise, and various specialty areas in the field, ask yourself:
"Who do I aspire to be like in 5 or 10 years?"
"Currently, who are the world's leading experts in the field?"

Try to learn from these people (i.e. what they know, what they do in business, where they speak/present). You may be surprised how quickly you learn from them. Over time you may become "that" person to another personal trainer.

Do your homework.
There are so many resources available to you to learn about fitness, exercise, nutrition, and business (in general). Dedicate time each day to gathering valuable information that will help you:
- Become a better personal trainer.
- Become a better business owner.
- Become a better marketer.
- Become a better sales person.

Mentors may be one of the best resources to draw upon for information, but be sure to respect their busy schedules and responsibilities to their own business.

Evolve your brand.
Continue to fine tune your unique personal brand (including your mission, vision and core values). Your clients will respect you more if you are genuine and effectively communicate your brand proposition as a way to accommodate their needs. Celebrate your strengths and recognize your weaknesses in an effort to better match your service offering to the right clients.

Do the work.
Some people may just get lucky and become incredibly successful without having to work very hard. For the 99 percent of us that live in the real world, this is not the case. Successful entrepreneurs (and successful people) generally work very hard (and in a smart way). What others may perceive as "luck" is merely the action they choose to take when an opportunity comes their way.

This is the first book in the "Business of Personal Training" series. For more information on upcoming topics and release dates, go to www.TodaysFitnessTrainer.com.

TESTIMONIALS

"When Andrea speaks, I listen. Carefully. She's a woman who has made a name in the industry as the consummate (and accomplished) professional while still managing to maintain a humility that belies her experience and abilities. I can't speak highly enough of her as a pioneer, a visionary, and an excellent human being.

If you want to understand how a successful personal training business should run, read this book. Twice. Just like a great movie has twists and turns you don't notice until the second viewing, this book contains concepts that will require further digestion before it can be assimilated. While we all may change and evolve as industry professionals, the words of wisdom contained within these pages are (in my opinion) timeless."

Jamie Atlas
Owner, Bonza Bodies Fitness

"Through this book, Andrea will help personal trainers take practical steps toward operating a "real" business. Specifically, trainers having left "employment" for a new journey in "entrepreneurship" will use this book as a resource to adopt essential business skills vital to success in the business of fitness."

Derek Curtice
Principal, Simplefit.net

"Although I have been in the Fitness industry for more than 30 years, I have yet to meet another fitness professional with the passion, creativity, commitment and vision as Andrea Oh. Her vision and guidance was instrumental in assisting me to create Canada's first interactive fitness and exergaming educational fitness facility. I consider Andrea a true friend and a real 'guru' in the industry.

Andrea's attention to detail and her insightful, supportive, and caring nature is rare. Fitness 4 Success' ability to host over 300 educational fitness field trips and over 600 birthday parties within a five year period could not have been done without Andrea's guidance and support. She supplied the framework and foundation for the business that I continue to implement to this day. I would strongly recommend that any fitness professional truly wanting to make a difference in the industry (with or without technology) take the time to connect with her first."

Noel Morgan
Owner, Fitness 4 Success Inc.
& President/CEO, Kater 2 Kids Fitness

"Andrea's passion for this topic is clearly visible in the content of this book. It is an all encompassing how-to guide for the uninitiated fitness neophyte, but also reinforces important information for the seasoned professional. In a world where we are inundated with information, it is comforting to know where to go for a clear, concise and practical guide to this wonderful career."

Rich Novelli
Chief Operating Officer, The Stadium

"Although I have been in the yoga business for over 8 years, I found new perspectives and many golden nuggets within the book that will undoubtedly improve my business! 'The Business of Personal Training' is an easy-to-follow roadmap to a successful career for entrepreneurs in the fitness industry!"

Lisa Sullivan
Regional Team Director, CorePower Yoga

"Andrea's expertise and knowledge greatly helped my Power Plate specialty fitness studio as we expanded our product and service offering. Her professionalism and exceptional ability to communicate clearly enabled her to efficiently direct our team through the various processes we needed implement to be more successful in business. This book is a direct reflection of her knowledge, expertise, and ability to help fitness professionals grow their business in record time!"

Graig Weisbart
Owner, Balance Point Fitness

Printed in Poland
by Amazon Fulfillment
Poland Sp. z o.o., Wrocław